THE SMOKE-FREE GUIDE

How to eliminate tobacco smoke
from your environment

Arlene Galloway

Qualy Publishing, Victoria, Canada

Geoff,
Thanks for your help & support,
Arlene

THE SMOKE-FREE GUIDE

How To Eliminate Tobacco Smoke
From Your Environment
By Arlene Galloway

Published by:

Qualy Publishing
Post Office Box 6399
Victoria, B.C. CANADA
V8P 5M3

Printed in Canada

Canadian Cataloguing in Publication Data
Galloway, Arlene, 1952-
The smoke-free guide : how to eliminate tobacco smoke from your environment

Includes bibliographical references and index.

ISBN 0-921348-02-9

1. Smoking - Prevention. 2. Smoking - Law and legislation. I. Title.
HV5733.G34 1988 363.1'9 C88-091208-1

Contents

Clearing the Air World-Wide

This book is dedicated to Dr. C. Everett Koop, Surgeon General of the United States, Jake Epp, Minister, National Health and Welfare, Canada, and Lynn McDonald, Member of Parliament, who have provided leadership in the pursuit of a smoke-free goal.

Acknowledgment

I would like to thank the following people for their assistance in providing information and reviewing the contents of a particular section of the book: Janet Chalupnik, Neil Collishaw, Herb Mills, Dr. John Read, Geoff Rowlands, Shirley Thompson, and Raymond Zoellick. In addition I would like to thank Gary Anderson, Bev Dobbyn, Dr. Bob Fisk, Susie Nute and Penny Pattison for their constructive criticism of specific chapters. I also acknowledge the encouragement and support I have received from many friends, relatives, colleagues and new acquaintances who have shared with me their experiences of exposure to environmental tobacco smoke.

This book has been produced by Dana Dahlquist of Spring Ridge Design (cover art), Lorraine Carter (editing), Ron Burr and his staff at Camera Ready Graphics (camera ready line copy and design), and Byron Johnson, sales representative, and the staff of Friesen Printers.

Introduction: Your Smoke-Free Goal

As more information becomes available about the contents of environmental tobacco smoke (ETS) and the health consequences of exposure to it, individuals have become very concerned about its existence in the air around them. The Surgeon General of the United States has recommended that exposure to ETS be eliminated and has stated that "it is imperative that parents eliminate tobacco smoke exposure from their child's environment."[1] Efforts are now being made by many people who smoke, and those who do not, to eliminate ETS from the air shared by them. This book can help you plan and achieve your own smoke-free goals.

If you are a person who smokes, in the following exercise you can add your frequency of exposure to mainstream smoke, which you breathe in directly from cigarettes, to your length of exposure to ETS. You may decide that in working towards a smoke-free goal for yourself or your family that you would like to quit smoking. Chapter 3 contains information on cessation methods and maintenance techniques which may be helpful to you in reaching your goal.

The first step in planning your goal is to determine where and when you and your family are exposed to ETS. It helps to log your exposure over a week-long period, including as well instances during the past year when unusual exposure took place. Possibly you visited or were visited by someone who smoked. You might prefer to look separately at the exposure of each member of your family, as the length of exposure for each may vary.

One person's assessment of her exposure is seen in Table 1. In that example, Jane Doe was exposed for an unusually long period of time during a visit in July with her mother.

In keeping track of your exposure, include any times when smoking occurs around you or you smell tobacco smoke. In situations where there is a central ventilation system, you may know that tobacco smoke is being circulated to your area although you cannot smell it. That could be included as part of your exposure time.

You may also want to add the level of exposure. This can be done on a subjective basis rating your exposure as light, moderate or heavy. For example, in an area where the air is

Table 1

Exposure to Environmental Tobacco Smoke Assessment Form

Name: Jane Doe

Day of the week	Place/Occasion	Length of Exposure (minutes)
Monday	at work where Jim & Janet smoke in my work area	420
	lunch time, sat with Sue in the smoking section of the restaurant	60
Tuesday	work	420
Wednesday	work	420
	rode to work with Brenda who smoked in the car	30
Thursday	work	420
	Bob and Linda came over for a visit and both smoked; took until Friday to get rid of the smell of smoke in my apartment	720
Friday	work	420
	theater lobby during intermission	20
Saturday	Party at John's where several people smoked indoors	300
Sunday	No exposure – free breathing day	0
Total exposure time during the week		3,230 (or 53.8 hours)

Infrequent exposure:

One week in July	Home and car; mother who smokes came to visit	7 days when indoors

blue with smoke and several people are smoking continuously, your exposure would be rated as heavy. Exposure to a higher level of ETS, as well as exposure over a longer period of time, may result in a higher risk of disease. However, no amount of exposure to ETS has been proven to be safe. Equipment to measure some of the chemicals which are part of ETS is available in some cities, but it has limited accuracy in measuring the low levels still considered to be toxic and cancer-producing. Because of the apparent lack of safety of any level of exposure, you should focus on whether or not you are exposed and the length of time you are exposed, rather than on the level of exposure.

Once you have determined where and when you and your family are exposed to ETS, decide what your first step will be in reaching a smoke-free goal. For example, Jane Doe may decide that her first step will be to make her home smoke-free. Or she might decide that she wants to first pursue a smoke-free work-place. In setting a goal, determine what you will accomplish and by when. The examples you will find in the book show that you will be more successful in reaching your goal if you take time to plan and discuss it. Therefore, in September, Jane might state: "My apartment will be a smoke-free area after December 1, and after that date anyone wishing to smoke at my home may do so on the balcony."

Once you have decided on your goal, plan the steps you will need to take to reach it successfully. Use the appropriate chapter of this book to help you plan your strategy. For example, Chapter 4 has ideas on how to make your home and car smoke-free. Chapter 5 gives 10 steps to follow to develop a work-place policy. These steps are explained in detail, including a section dealing with work-places which are also public places. Later in this chapter, the process the Insurance Corporation of British Columbia followed to develop its policy is described, using the 10 steps as an outline. A copy of the memorandum used by the corporation to communicate information about the policy to its staff is found in Appendix B. The special case of hospital policies is dealt with at the end of Chapter 5 using Swedish Hospital Medical Center in Seattle, Washington as an example.

Where you and your family are exposed to ETS in community settings, your goal may be related to a local ordinance or bylaw. The 10 steps taken to make the Vancouver

City bylaw a reality are covered in Chapter 7, and a rating of the resulting bylaw is given.

If your concerns about ETS extend to the regional or national level, Chapter 8 explains what is happening now in the United States and Canada. Suggestions for individual and group action are included. This chapter also contains a rating of the Washington State Clean Indoor Air Act, with a rating scale that you can apply to a state or provincial law to determine how much protection it provides against exposure to ETS.

Chapter 9 takes a look at the tobacco issue in developing countries and the recommendations made by the World Health Organization and the delegates to the Sixth World Conference on Smoking and Health. You may find some ideas for your own goal among these recommendations.

A new area of nonsmoking promotion is occurring with the linking of nonsmoking with sports activities. Chapter 10 describes the development of the Fresh Air Program for the XV Olympic Games.

These are just some of the ways you might choose to promote nonsmoking and decrease your exposure to environmental tobacco smoke:

- Have a smoke-free home and car.
- Encourage your friends to have smoke-free homes and cars.
- Always ask to be seated in a nonsmoking section at restaurants, or preferably, eat at restaurants which are smoke-free.
- Use smoke-free hotel and motel rooms and smoke-free rental cars when travelling.
- Fly on nonsmoking flights whenever these are available and request that all flights be smoke-free.
- Travel on smoke-free buses.
- Ask professionals you visit, for example dentists and doctors, to have a "no smoking" policy in their offices.
- Propose "no smoking" policy resolutions for meetings and events held by organizations in which you and/or your family have membership.
- Promote smoke-free policies for local schools and child-care facilities.
- When asked by people if you mind if they smoke, let them know that you do mind because you do not want to be exposed to ETS.

- Initiate a smoke-free policy in your work-place.
- Join groups which are working toward smoke-free policies in your work-place or in public places in your community.
- Let car dealers know what optional uses could be made of the ashtray space in cars and how the design of the space could accommodate these uses.
- Compliment businesses which provide you with a smoke-free environment and ask others, in writing, to supply one in the future.
- Request that local schools and day-care centers have smoke-free policies and provide smoking prevention programs to children and young adults.
- Write to elected officials (municipal, state/provincial or national representatives) from your area, commending them for their stand to promote smoke-free spaces or asking them to initiate and/or support laws and regulations to promote nonsmoking (see Chapter 9 for recommendations which have been made internationally).
- Promote the effectiveness of local ordinances and bylaws by being aware of their coverage and reporting noncompliance.
- Give financial support and/or volunteer time to health organizations and other groups which promote nonsmoking.

Part of your plan to reach your goal may be to obtain more information. The information in Chapters 1 and 2, and in Appendix A will help you become more knowledgeable about the health consequences of tobacco use and exposure to ETS. Appendix C offers you information on where you might get assistance and support to reach your goal. Many of these national organizations also have offices and staff at the local and regional levels. Most are listed in your telephone directory. These local resources may be more accessible to you and may have all the information you need. As well, the staff may be able to offer you consulting services to help you reach your own particular goal.

By promoting nonsmoking, you can help eliminate environmental tobacco smoke not only from your home but also from where you work, shop, play, and otherwise spend time indoors. It is important to learn about ETS and the known and potential effects of exposure to it. Only when you have the facts can you determine the value of eliminating ETS exposure for you and your family.

It is also important to realize that smoking is an addictive behavior. Many people find it difficult to quit. On the other hand, you make this addiction more socially acceptable – to children as well as adults – if you allow it in your environment. In a way, you are making it harder for the many people who smoke and want to quit if you allow them to smoke around you. One of the reasons that so many people are addicted to tobacco is that it is so easy to start smoking. Not only has the substance been readily available but society has also encouraged its use. To eliminate ETS from the environment of people who do not actively smoke, it is now necessary to provide environments where smoking does not occur.

Once you have reached your initial goal, you may want to continue to promote nonsmoking by setting a new goal. As more people become involved in the many levels of nonsmoking promotion, a smoke-free goal will be more easily attained.

Source:
1. Remarks by C. Everett Koop, Surgeon General of the United States, at a press conference releasing the 1986 Surgeon General's Report on **The Health Consequences of Involuntary Smoking**, December 16, 1986.

FIRST THE FACTS

"Smoking is a social disorder involving the inhalation of addictive toxic chemicals that ultimately cause premature death from heart disease, cancer and respiratory disease in about 50 percent of smokers... The evidence that ...exposure [to the toxic chemicals in tobacco smoke] is capable of causing disease in nonsmokers is solid and rapidly increasing."
Repace, J.L. "Passive smoking has no place in the work-place." **Canadian Medical Association Journal.** 133(8):738, October 15,1985.

Figure 1. The internationally recognized "no smoking" symbol — a red circle and diagonal slash superimposed on an illustration of a burning cigarette. Courtesy of the British Columbia Lung Association.

Chapter 1 : Health Consequences of Tobacco Use

With many diseases, the reasons why some people become ill and others do not remain largely unknown. We can only look at the disease-related factors that we can identify to try to determine which ones are important. Some common causes which have been identified in the past include contaminated water, poor shelter, lack of nutritious food, and lack of cleanliness. Not all people who drink contaminated water or who have poor shelter or who have poor hygiene will feel ill, but their level of health (ability to do physical exercise, perform mental work, and feel well) is more likely to be lower than that of those who are not exposed to these problems, and the risk of them actually becoming ill is higher.

In some areas of the world the problems with water, shelter, food, and sanitation still exist, but more modern problems now affect levels of health and cause disease in the more affluent countries. These modern problems, some of which may also compound existing problems in poorer areas and Third World countries, are often related to lifestyle choices. One example of a lifestyle choice which affects health is cigarette smoking.

The risk of disease has to be kept in perspective. Not everyone who smokes will die of lung cancer, heart disease or some other disease related to cigarette smoking. Similarily, not everyone who does not smoke will escape these diseases, although it is rare for a nonsmoker to develop lung cancer, for example. It is not a clear case of black and white, or known consequences following specific actions – the fact that you smoke does not mean you will die before the age of 65 years.

Although most, if not all, people who smoke will accumulate tar in their lungs and suffer some health consequences because of their smoking habit, not all will find these effects on their health to be a problem. Many of the effects accumulate slowly over years of smoking (for example, the need to walk or run more slowly because of lack of breath, or the occurrence of coughing spells in the morning), so they may be attributed to advancing age rather than the true cause.

Many people who smoke will have poorer health because of their habit, but will not actually be ill. Others who smoke will, due to both known and unknown factors, become ill and some of them will die prematurely. Premature death occurs when a person dies before the average life expectancy, which for men in the United States is 70 years and in Canada is 70.2 years. The equivalent figures for women are 77.8 years in the United States and 77.5 years in Canada.[1] To give conservative estimates of life years lost because of early death, many studies base their results on a life expectancy of 65 years. What scientists have shown is that people who smoke are more likely to die prematurely from a variety of illnesses than people who do not smoke. When this is found to be true, it is stated that the "risk" of the disease is greater for those who smoke. This increased risk of early death for people who smoke is reflected in the 50 percent higher cost of premiums they pay for term life insurance for some policies.

For some diseases, the likelihood of illness and/or death is much higher for people who smoke than for nonsmokers, and no other individual factor has been found to have as great an influence on disease occurrence. In these cases, the factor is considered to be a major cause of the disease. This is true of cigarette smoking and lung cancer – 85 percent of lung cancer is felt to be attributable to cigarette smoking.

This 85 percent is called the fraction of lung cancer attributable to smoking. As more diseases are associated with smoking, each is being studied to find out what fraction of the disease could be prevented by eliminating smoking in the population. In 1984, 315,120 deaths from a variety of causes were attributed to smoking in the United States. In Canada, the number of deaths per year would be approximately one-tenth of the U.S. total.

Table 2 includes many of the causes of death associated with smoking, and the number of deaths from each disease which were attributed to smoking in the United States in 1984. For some of these diseases, only a small percentage of the total deaths are attributed to smoking. For example, only 13 percent of the 5,245 deaths from sudden infant death syndrome in the United States in 1984 were attributed to smoking. For other diseases, a large proportion of the deaths are related to smoking. For example, 85 percent of men and 69 percent of the women who die from chronic airways obstruction do so because of smoking. Table 2 does not include deaths from peripheral vascular disease, cancer at unspecified sites, cigarette-caused fires, or deaths of nonsmokers due to exposure to environmental tobacco smoke.

Many studies have been done to determine the risks of disease associated with the use of tobacco, especially in the form of cigarettes. This world wide research has been reviewed and summarized annually in the United States. Section 8(a) of the Public Health Cigarette Smoking Act of 1969 mandates that a report be written to Congress each year on the health consequences of smoking. Information from these Surgeon Generals' reports since 1980 are found in Appendix A, in a true-false statement format.

Source:
1. Grant, M. **Handbook of Community Health.** (Fourth Edition). Lea and Febiger: Philadelphia, 1987, p.21.

Table 2

Total Number of Deaths Attributable to Smoking, by Disease Category and Sex : United States, 1984

Disease Category	Males	Females	Total
Adults 20 years old and over			
Cancers			
Lip, mouth, throat	3,958	1,110	5,068
Esophagus	3,717	1,257	4,974
Stomach	1,455	1,467	2,922
Pancreas	3,459	1,653	5,112
Larynx (voice box)	2,385	274	2,660
Trachea, lung, bronchus	65,659	27,170	92,829
Cervix	0	1,685	1,685
Urinary bladder	2,447	853	3,299
Kidney, other urinary	1,319	403	1,722
Circulatory diseases			
High blood pressure	2,099	2,645	4,744
Ischemic heart disease (e.g., heart attack) at less than age 65	22,362	4,892	27,253
Ischemic heart disease at age 65 and over	33,461	16,816	50,276
Cardiac arrest (sudden stopping of the heart)	7,745	5,950	13,695
Cerebrovascular disease (e.g., strokes)	5,692	12,228	17,920
Arteriosclerosis (hardening of the arteries)	2,200	4,797	6,996
Aortic aneurysm	6,444	2,244	8,689
Respiratory diseases			
Pneumonia, influenza	5,986	2,679	8,664
Chronic bronchitis and emphysema	9,097	3,831	12,928
Chronic airways obstruction	26,541	11,545	38,085
Digestive diseases			
Ulcers	1,556	1,497	3,053
Diseases of children, less than 1 year of age			
Premature delivery, low birthweight	314	279	593
Respiratory distress syndrome	396	251	647
Other respiratory conditions of the newborn	360	275	636
Sudden infant death syndrome	405	264	669
Total	209,057	106,063	315,120

Source: U.S. Department of Health and Human Services. "Smoking-Attributable Mortality and Years of Potential Life Lost : United States, 1984." **Centers for Disease Control Morbidity and Mortality Weekly Report.** 36(42):693-697, October 30, 1987.

Chapter 2 : Environmental Tobacco Smoke (ETS)

Compared to the number of studies on the health consequences of active smoking (50,000), the number on the consequences of exposure to ETS are few (several hundred).[1] However, these studies are gradually showing evidence of the negative effects on health related to this type of exposure. It should be remembered that when studies of active smoking began, the evidence related to lung cancer was at first sketchy, and then grew until few people will now dispute that cigarette smoking is a major cause of lung cancer. Also, the list of illnesses related to active smoking is still growing. Only after many more studies have been done will we have a more complete picture of the health consequences of exposure to ETS.

What is ETS?

Environmental tobacco smoke is a combination of smoke exhaled by people who smoke (or exhaled mainstream smoke), and smoke which is produced at the lit end of a cigarette or other burned tobacco product (sidestream smoke).

ETS contains at least 3800 chemicals, of which over 50 are known cancer-causing substances in animals, humans, or both.[2] The burning of unknown additives and flavorings, especially in low tar[3] and nicotine cigarettes, may add to this number of chemicals. The health effects of many of these substances are unknown.

Some substances with common names which are found in ETS include formaldehyde, carbon monoxide, hydrogen cyanide, ammonia, nicotine, aniline, naphthalene, and arsenic.[4] Many of these substances are allowed only at restricted levels in industry since exposure to them has been shown to cause illness.

It is known that the concentration of many of the hazardous chemicals is higher in sidestream smoke than in mainstream smoke. About 300 to 400 of the more than 3800 chemicals found in tobacco smoke have been measured in both mainstream and sidestream smoke. Much higher levels of ammonia, nitrogen oxide, and the highly carcinogenic N-nitrosamines are found in sidestream smoke.[5]

Sidestream smoke from filtered cigarettes contains high levels of NDMA (N-nitrosodimethylamine), one of the most potent animal carcinogens known. According to standards for industrial exposure, avoidance of exposure to NDMA is recommended. There is no safe level assigned to this substance. A person exposed to air heavily contaminated with ETS may inhale as much NDMA in one hour as an active smoker would by inhaling the mainstream smoke of up to 35 filter-tipped cigarettes. This is because the filter removes most of the NDMA from mainstream smoke and increases the concentration in the sidestream smoke.[6] Sidestream smoke also contains higher levels of pyridines, hydrogen cyanide, carbon monoxide, acrolein and benzene.[7]

Standards have been set for safe levels of a variety of chemicals. These standards are considered when looking at safety and health, for example, in industry.[8] According to these standards, both sidestream and mainstream smoke contain at least two cancer-causing chemicals that are not considered safe at any level. These two substances are beta naphthylamine and 4-aminobiphenyl. Both of the substances are found in higher concentrations in sidesteam smoke than in mainstream smoke.[9] It is interesting to note that where a company allows these substances to be present in areas in which employees work, the company could be considered in violation of industry standards. However, in the case of these substances being present as part of ETS, these chemicals are often, in fact, being introduced by the employees themselves.

Standards have been set for only some of the thousands of substances in ETS. Tobacco smoke itself, which is too complex to study in its entirety, has not been assigned a "safe" level. It is known that individually many of the substances it contains are dangerous to health. It is unknown how the interactions of these many substances together affect health. At this point, we can only go by standards which have been set for individual substances found in ETS.

Nonsmokers who are regularly exposed to environmental tobacco smoke absorb between one percent and 20 percent of the cancer-causing and toxic substances absorbed by people who actively smoke.[10]

Is ventilation practical?

The use of increased ventilation is usually not practical because of the costs involved in heating or cooling the fresh air brought into the system. Also, the air exchange necessary would overwhelm a ventilation system. It is estimated that to keep the level of respirable suspended particles (RSPs) below the recommended level, where one person is smoking in a small room, it would be necessary to exchange the air over 100 times every hour. This rate is much greater than that found in office buildings and homes.[11] This level of ventilation would still not remove the gaseous portion of ETS which also contains toxic and cancer-causing substances.

The particles found in ETS are extremely small and quickly disperse in the air. Many nonsmokers are exposed to this ETS which can contribute substantially to indoor air pollution.[12]

One practical way to eliminate exposure to ETS is to provide separate indoor areas for people who smoke, and for those who do not, and make sure that the areas are not only physically separate, but also that the ventilation systems of the areas are entirely separate. A more effective way to eliminate exposure is to prohibit smoking in the indoor area.[13]

Health Consequences

The most common immediate effects of exposure to ETS are irritation of the eyes, nose and throat, and reactions to the smell. An adverse reaction to the odour is a more sensitive indicator of the presence of ETS than the level of irritation.[14]

Cotinine, a by-product of nicotine, is found in the urine of infants and other nonsmokers when exposed to tobacco smoke.[15] It has been reported that mothers who are nonsmokers, but who are exposed to ETS, either at work or at home, for at least two hours per day during pregnancy, produce babies with a lower birthweight than babies whose mothers did not have this exposure to ETS. This kind of exposure doubles the nonsmokers' risk of having a growth-retarded infant.[16]

A few studies have indicated that children with parents who smoke grow and develop more slowly than children of nonsmoking parents. Wheezing, coughing and sputum (or phlegm) production are more common in children of parents who smoke than in children of nonsmokers. Pneumonia and bronchitis are also more common. There is some evidence that children of parents who smoke have a slower rate of lung growth. In several studies it has been found that children of parents who smoke have an increased risk of chronic ear infections.[17]

Children exposed to ETS because of their parents' smoking habits are, in general, sicker than children whose parents do not smoke. Exposure to ETS results in more days of restricted activity, more days in bed and more hospitalizations for these children.[18]

People with chronic diseases such as heart disease, lung disease and allergies to other substances can experience increased problems when exposed to ETS. Exposure to ETS causes an increase in heart rate and blood pressure and can reduce the amount of exercise a person with heart disease can do before experiencing chest pain. Similarily, people with lung disease, when exposed to ETS, develop shortness of breath more quickly when exercising. People with allergies to other substances find ETS more irritating to their eyes, nose and throat than those without allergies.[19] Studies of children with asthma have indicated that exposure to ETS from parental smoking aggravates the children's health problem.[20]

Recent studies have indicated that exposure to ETS can also cause decreased lung function, decreased driving ability, headaches, nausea, and dizziness as well as increase a person's risk of bronchitis, pneumonia and other respiratory infections which in turn lead to more days of disability. The long-term effects of exposure to ETS may also include a decrease in the functioning of the small airways of the respiratory tract, and a higher risk of heart disease and cancers of the nasal sinuses, breast, cervix, endocrine glands, and leukemia, Hodgkin's disease and other lymphomas.[21] More studies need to be done to either confirm or disprove recent findings which have linked these illnesses to ETS.

Preliminary studies are also showing a link between parents who smoke and an increased risk of cancer in their adult children. One study of people with cancer between the ages of 15 and 59 years showed that a person whose father smoked had a 50 percent greater chance of getting cancer. Cancers associated with blood-making processes, like leukemia, were found more frequently in children whose mother and father smoked.[22]

There is some concern that when a person inhales the decay products of radon found in ETS (like bone-seeking lead-210), these products may end up in the skeleton, especially in growing children, and may result in irradiation of the bone marrow. Adults would be less sensitive to this radiation than children. More studies need to be done to see if there is a link between this type of irradiating substance found in ETS and certain types of cancers like leukemia. Although these results are preliminary, the skeletons of adults who smoke have been found to contain higher levels of lead-210.[23]

At the annual meeting of the American Heart Foundation in 1987, researchers reported that a study of 11- and 12-year-old boys showed that boys whose parents smoked had thicker heart walls, stiffer aortas (the main artery coming from the heart), and lower levels of "good" cholesterol. This indicates that sons of parents who smoke may have a higher risk of heart disease later in their lives.[24] These findings show that there may be long-term effects of exposure to ETS that we have not yet identified.

Studies on nonsmoking spouses of people who smoke indicate that exposure to ETS significantly increases the risk of lung cancer. This risk is estimated to be 10 to 300 percent higher in nonsmoking spouses of smokers compared to nonsmoking spouses of nonsmokers.[25]

Exposure to environmental tobacco smoke, in most instances, does not subject an individual to the same level of poisonous and cancer-causing substances as active smoking, since the smoke tends to be diluted somewhat in the air. However, we now know that people who do not actively smoke but are exposed to environmental tobacco smoke can suffer from illnesses related to this exposure. We also know that ETS can make some pre-existing illnesses much worse. As yet, we do not know how many illnesses are related to exposure to ETS, nor do we know how widespread and extensive the effects of exposure to ETS are in the population.

It may be that all of the health consequences of active smoking are to be found in people exposed to ETS, albeit at a less frequent rate and/or a less serious level of illness. It may also be true that exposure to ETS causes, or increases the risk of, illnesses not associated with active smoking. These are more likely to be found as a result of exposure of very young children who may have ETS-related illnesses later in life. Further research will give us more clues about the effects of ETS in the population but it would seem prudent at this time to limit, or eliminate, exposure to environmental tobacco smoke.

Sources:

1. United States Public Health Service. **The Health Consequences of Involuntary Smoking. A Report of the Surgeon General.** U. S. Department of Health and Human Services: Washington, D.C., 1986.

2. Collishaw, N.E., Kirkbride and Wigle. "Tobacco smoke in the workplace: an occupational health hazard."**Canadian Medical Association Journal.** 131(10):1199, November 15, 1984.

3. ETS consists of gases and particles. When nicotine and water have been removed from the particles, the remaining substance is referred to as "tar". This tar consists of a wide variety of cancer-causing polycyclic aromatic hydrocarbons, phenols, cresols, naphthols, alkanes and alkenes, benzenes, naphthalenes, carboxylic acids, metallic ions, radioactive compounds, agricultural chemicals, and additives.
United States Public Health Service. **Smoking and Health. A Report of the Surgeon General.** U.S. Department of Health and Human Services: Washington, D.C., 1979, p.1-29.

4. Dewey, M. **Smoke in the Workplace — An Action Manual for Nonsmokers.** Nonsmokers' Rights Association:Toronto, Canada, 1985, pp.74-76.

5. National Research Council. **Environmental Tobacco Smoke — Measuring Exposures and Assessing Health Effects.** National Academy Press: Washington, D.C., 1986.

6. Wigle, D. "Tobacco Smoke and the Nonsmoker." **Chronic Diseases in Canada.** 3(1):5, June 1982.
7. National Research Council, pp.28-35.
8. American Conference of Governmental Industrial Hygienists. **Threshold Limit Values for Chemical Substances and Physical Agents in the Workroom Environment with Intended Changes for 1983-84.** Cincinnati, Ohio, 1983.
9. National Program to Reduce Tobacco Use: Consultation, Planning and Implementation Committee. **Directional Paper of the National Program to Reduce Tobacco Use in Canada.** Health and Welfare Canada: Ottawa, June 1987, p.8.
10. Wigle, D.T., Collishaw and Kirkbride. "Exposure of involuntary smokers to toxic components of tobacco smoke." **Canadian Journal of Public Health.** 78(3):153, May/June 1987.
11. Wigle, D. "Tobacco Smoke and the Nonsmoker," p.6.
12. United States Public Health Service. Surgeon General's Report, 1986.
13. Repace, J.L. and Lowrey. "An indoor air quality standard for ambient tobacco smoke based on carcinogenic risk."**New York State Journal of Medicine.** 85(7):381, July 1985.
14. Environmental Health Directorate. **Involuntary Exposure to Tobacco Smoke.** (87-EHD-138) Health and Welfare Canada: Ottawa, 1987, pp.7-8.
15. Woodward, A. et al. "Cotinine in urine of smokers' infants" (letter) **Lancet.** 2(8408):935, October 20, 1984.
16. Martin, T.R. and Bracken. "Association of low birth weight with passive smoke exposure in pregnancy." **American Journal of Epidemiology.** 124 (4):633-642, October 1986.
17. National Research Council, pp. 7-12.
18. Glantz, S.A. "Health effects of ambient tobacco smoke."in Walsh, P.J. et al (editors). **Indoor Air Quality.** CRC Press, Inc.: Boca Raton, Florida, 1984, p.168.
19. Glantz, S.A., pp.169,170.
20. Environmental Health Directorate, p.8
21. Collishaw, N.E. **Involuntary Exposure to Tobacco Smoke.** Paper presented to the Fourth Environmental Government Affairs Seminar, Ottawa, Ontario, October 21, 1986.
22. Sandler, D.P. et al. "Cancer risk in adulthood from early life exposure to parents' smoking."**American Journal of Public Health.** 75(5):487-492, May 1985.
23. National Research Council, p. 255.

24. "Boys' hearts suffer from stiffer arteries if parents smoke." **Victoria Times-Colonist.** November 19, 1987, p.B14.
25. United States Public Health Service, Surgeon General's Report, 1986. p. 97.

CLEARING THE AIR
IN YOUR PERSONAL ENVIRONMENT

"The evidence on the composition of tobacco smoke and on the health hazards of involuntary exposure suggests that there may not be a "safe" level for such exposure."

Collishaw, N.E., Kirkbride and Wigle. "Tobacco smoke in the work-place: an occupational health hazard." **Canadian Medical Association Journal.** 131(10):1199, November 15, 1984.

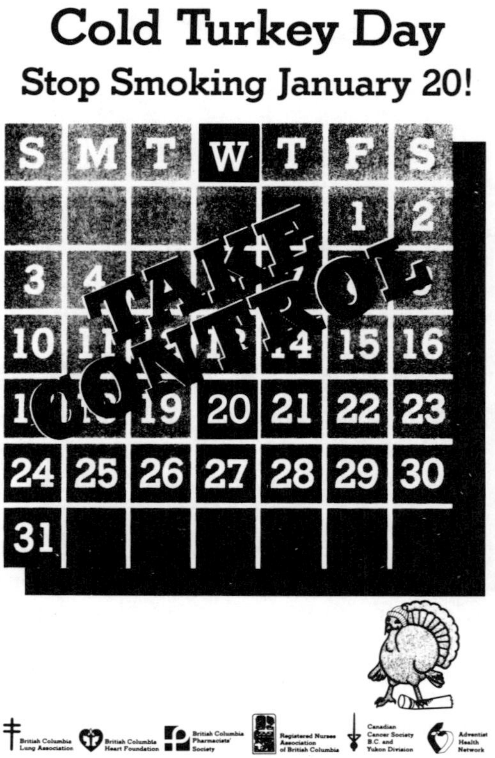

Figure 2. Example of sign to encourage cessation used in British Columbia in 1988.

Chapter 3 : Cessation Methods, or How to Quit

For those who want to quit smoking, there are a variety of methods available, none of which is always successful. People who succeed in their attempt to quit smoking must be committed to stopping. This commitment can be made stronger if they believe that the dangers to health are personally relevant to them and/or if they have compelling reasons to quit. Many people try to quit several times before they succeed. Success appears to be more likely if a variety of cessation methods are used together and the person truly believes that he or she will be able to quit.

The Methods

The following information is listed in alphabetical order.

Acupuncture

This method is based on the Chinese science of connections within the human body and makes use of needles or staple-like attachments for treatment. One method, nasopuncture, consists of selecting points on the surface of the nose to decongest the person's respiratory tract and to make the person dislike tobacco. Another method, auriculopuncture, uses press needles or staple puncture in one ear. Some acupuncturists are using other points; for example on the wrist.

A new form of acupuncture uses lasers. Typical points used are the ear, nose and a spot between the thumb and index finger. One practitioner offering this type of service treats the client once every week for three weeks. Treatment schedules may vary with the practitioner and the client.

Behavioral Methods

These methods use either punishment, which includes aversive procedures like rapid smoking or shock therapy, or positive rewards, which include self-management procedures like desensitization and relaxation, nicotine fading, and behavioral rehearsal.

Counselling and Support

Health professionals may overestimate what their clients know about the dangers of smoking. Effective counselling by physicians or other health professionals, along with support of friends and family, will improve the likelihood of success in quitting smoking.

Educational approaches, Clinics and Groups

Non-profit clinic and group programs usually have low fees, trained leaders and an emphasis on health education. Many of these programs are provided through cancer, lung, and heart associations.

Some commercial smoking cessation programs also exist and these tend to have higher fees. Many of these can be found advertised in the Yellow Pages in your local telephone directory. Others are travelling seminars advertised in community newspapers.

Hypnosis

Treatment may consist of one or more individual sessions or group treatments. Many hypnotists use suggestions, imagery, relaxation and self-hypnosis to supplement their treatment. Follow-up support is useful for the person to remain free of smoking.

Mass Media Programs

Many people can be reached by the use of television and radio. Television can play an important beginning role in changing a person's self-perception from that of a smoker to that of a nonsmoker.

Medication

None of the drugs, except nicotine chewing gum, that have been tested for use in smoking cessation (for example clonidine, lobeline, meprobamate) have been found to work well.

Nicorette (a brand name for nicotine chewing gum) is a prescription drug in the form of a sugar-free gum which contains nicotine. As yet there has been little research to determine if persons using nicotine chewing gum as an aid to smoking cessation remain off tobacco once they quit using the gum. The nicotine from the gum is absorbed into the body more slowly than from smoking and will not duplicate the effect of cigarettes. If the gum is not chewed properly the side effects may increase. The side effects, which are related to either the nicotine or to gum chewing, include irritation in the mouth, problems with dental work, aching jaw muscles, indigestion, excessive salivation, insomnia, dizziness, irritability, headache, lack of appetite, and hiccups.

People who have had recent heart attacks, are pregnant or breastfeeding, have severe or worsening chest pain or serious irregular heart rhythms, or have disease in their jaw joint, should not use nicotine chewing gum. Those with inflamed areas in their mouth or throat or who have a history of inflammation of the esophagus or stomach ulcers should use it with caution. Nicotine chewing gum may be used by people who are highly motivated to quit smoking and who use it to help decrease withdrawal symptoms while using another smoking cessation method.

If you are using nicotine gum, remember that it is a drug and that it should be kept out of the reach of children. Otherwise, a child may find the gum and treat it as candy. A child who has chewed and/or swallowed some of the gum should receive immediate medical attention.

Self-Care

Quitting "cold turkey", an example of self-care where the person abruptly stops smoking on his or her own, has been used successfully by more people than any other form of cessation. Self-care includes activities where the person: develops a personal method of quitting; receives brief instructions on how to quit and then follows instructions; or uses an aid or self-help guide (for example, book, booklet, record, cassette, filter, lozenges, videotape, drug store preparation, or information received by mail).

Ingredients for Success

A person is more likely to be successful in quitting smoking if he or she:

- is motivated to quit and can turn the wish to quit into the decision to quit;
- expects to succeed and not be smoking after a year;
- has friends and family who support his or her attempt to quit;
- has worked out strategies to cope with the urge to smoke;
- takes personal responsibility to quit and wants to quit for his or her own purposes and not because someone else thought it was a good idea;
- is not in a period of high stress after initial quitting (for example, quitting just before Christmas is often difficult because of the pressure to smoke at social gatherings);
- agrees that smoking is a health risk (the presence of illness may increase the person's motivation to quit);
- uses a combination of cessation methods which he or she feels will be most successful;
- uses a method of quitting that involves some cost to increase the motivation to quit; and
- has planned some good maintenance strategies which will help to deal with the effects of the former addiction, are tailored to personal needs and interests, and will provide continuing, long-term support.

Cessation consists of three sequential steps:

- Preparation

If a person believes that there are risks associated with continued smoking and that there are benefits in quitting, motivation to quit increases. That person will feel more confident of success.

- Intervention

The person becomes actively involved in his or her own cessation program and actually quits smoking; and

- Maintenance

This is the key to successful long-term smoking cessation and includes social support and the use of substitutes like exercise and other coping strategies tailored to an individual's needs and interests.

The main factor involved in breaking the smoking habit is successful maintenance. Many people who initially quit smoking, either on their own or with assistance, begin smoking again. This usually occurs when the person is under social pressure to smoke, is coping with negative emotional stress or is coping with conflict in a relationship. Smoking one cigarette often leads to full-time smoking. People who quit successfully on their own appear to use the increased knowledge and skill they have acquired from previous efforts to quit.

Each individual must learn to deal with urges and pressures to smoke, as this is essential to lasting success. The success rate of any cessation method depends on whether or not the method is acceptable to the individual and includes well-planned maintenance strategies.

Maintenance Strategies

Social Support

Social support can provide continuing motivation to the exsmoker and can supplement the person's own ability to change his or her behavior to that of a person who does not smoke, and to maintain this change. Those in the immediate environment can provide significant support to the person who has quit smoking. Friends, family, co-workers, health-care professionals, persons providing a smoking cessation program, or a self-help group can all play a part. A smoke-free environment, both at home and at work, can be a positive influence in supporting a person's decision to quit.

One method of support in some cessation programs is the use of buddies, where two or more clients provide support to each other over the telephone. A problem may occur with this plan if one buddy starts to smoke again. It is easier to maintain a buddy system in the work-place setting where buddies can meet face to face to provide support to each other over a prolonged period of time.

The exsmoker may wish to involve a close family member or friend in drawing up a verbal or written contract to aid in maintenance. This could include, for instance, the exsmoker writing a check for an amount which is significant to the exsmoker and which is to benefit a cause to which he or she is opposed. The friend or family member then keeps the check and will send it in only if the person starts to smoke again.

The use of feedback on improved lung function (either through medical tests or personal observation techniques such as gradually increasing the speed of stair-climbing without having breathing problems) may be useful to the exsmoker. Social support strategies which may be used in the work-place include incentives like cash bonuses, prizes, extra vacation time, praise from management and co-workers, bets, competitions and employer recognition.

Coping Skills

Exsmokers need skill in coping with the urge to smoke. First, they need to identify situations that are high-risk for them – that is, which situations are most likely to be the ones in which he or she will want to smoke. Next the person can rehearse a response to these situations by role-playing with someone else or by simply thinking it out. This rehearsal can increase confidence in dealing with high-risk situations. Once a person has quit smoking, it helps to take just one day at a time and count each day of success.

It is important not to let one slip become a total return to the previous smoking behavior. If a person smokes one or more cigarettes, the situation in which the smoking occurred must be examined to decide how it could be handled differently the next time or how this type of situation could be avoided for a period of time. The person needs to continue to believe that he or she can, and will, quit successfully.

The exsmoker may find maintenance is made easier through increasing knowledge and skill related to exercise, nutrition and relaxation. Exercise and/or relaxation techniques like deep breathing exercises can be used to replace tobacco, for those who used tobacco to try to decrease stress. Attention to a balanced diet can help to decrease the effects of nicotine withdrawal and the likelihood of long-term weight gain for the person who has quit smoking.

Another useful coping strategy is the use of self-rewards. These, as well as a balanced diet, relaxation and exercise, can help the person to cope with the physical and emotional symptoms which sometimes occur during the months following cessation of smoking. The exsmoker, perhaps together with friends and family members, can decide on rewards for various lengths of time of cessation or after successfully coping with a high-risk situation. For example, after the first day without smoking, the person might go out to dinner with a friend (in the nonsmoking section of a restaurant). After one week, the person may decide a reward of a movie or a special dessert is in order. The person can continue to use rewards after specific lengths of time or after handling a high-risk situation successfully. Larger rewards may be planned after quitting successfully for three months, six months and one year. The rewards must be meaningful for the individual so that they can be anticipated with excitement and provide motivation to remain an exsmoker. It may be important to consider rewards which only expose the person to an environment that is free of tobacco smoke.

Preparing Mentally for Relapses

The exsmoker needs to be able to recognize situations where a slip may occur and develop a strategy to cope with a relapse if it happens. This is important to minimize the impact of a slip and to prevent a full-blown return to smoking. Before quitting a person must begin to develop an identity as a nonsmoker and expect success in quitting. A continuation of this process will help the person deal successfully with slips if they occur.

Leading causes of relapses are anxiety, stress, anger, frustration, social pressures, weight gain, and low self-esteem. Situations where the person is feeling positive can also lead to a relapse. This often occurs when the person is eating, with people who smoke, and/or drinking coffee or alcohol.

After breaking the habit of smoking, a person still has to deal with the long-term effects of the former addiction, which include tolerance to the drug and dependence. Craving for cigarettes is a major cause of relapse because intense emotions of any kind tend to be experienced as a craving for the drug. Remaining free of tobacco depends in part on the person's ability to resolve life's problems and to gain satisfaction and pleasure by means other than addictive smoking. A person's intention to quit smoking represents a major life decision — an addiction is being left behind and replaced with more natural and socially acceptable ways of finding enjoyment. The exsmoker can experience a sense of new-found freedom and pride in taking control of that part of his or her life that was previously controlled by an addiction to nicotine.

The following reference, used to compile the information in this chapter on cessation methods, ingredients for success, and maintenance strategies is an excellent source of information for anyone wanting further information on cessation.

Source:
Schwartz, Jerome L. **Review and Evaluation of Smoking Cessation Methods: The United States and Canada, 1978-1985**. (National Institutes of Health Publication No. 87-2940) Division of Cancer Prevention and Control, National Cancer Institute and the U.S. Department of Health and Human Services: Washington, D.C., April 1987.

Resources for Smoking Cessation

Information on smoking cessation methods available in your area, including specialized programs for adolescents and pregnant women, may be obtained through your public health department or local offices of the national health organizations listed in Appendix C. You may also find books and audiocassettes on the subject at your local library or bookstore.

Programs offered privately by individual practitioners (for example, hypnotists and acupuncturists) and private companies and organizations are often found under "Smokers' Information and Treatment Centers" in the Yellow Pages of your telephone directory. Your physician may also be willing to provide individual counselling and advice about programs and other information which may be useful to you.

Chapter 4 : At Home and in Your Car

For the sake of courtesy, many people who do not smoke permit smoking in their homes and cars, while resenting the fact that they are being exposed to the nuisance and health problems related to environmental tobacco smoke. Other nonsmokers openly ridicule or harass smokers about their behavior. Either way, people who smoke have a problem. Either they cause ill feeling, sometimes unknowingly, or they are badgered because of an addictive behavior they have either been unable to quit, or do not want to quit.

For most of our social behavior, there are unwritten rules which we follow. We learned these rules as we were growing up, or later from our friends and other influential people in our lives. Changes in social norms (or what is accepted as normal or average in our society) usually occur over a number of years or even decades. The rules associated with the behavior of smoking are changing more rapidly as more people become aware of the health hazards of exposure to ETS and are no longer able to ignore its potential effects. On the other hand, they see that some of their friends and relatives have difficulty in stopping their addictive behavior for several hours at a time.

Because social norms are changing quickly, there is a need for people to establish rules for smoking in their home and cars. Rules for a household should be the same for everyone. Discussion should include how others who visit the home or

Figure 3. Two samples of smoke-free car signs. Courtesy of the British Columbia Lung Association and the Canadian Council on Smoking and Health.

use the car will be made aware of the rules for tobacco smoking.

Choose Rules for Your Household

Generally the basic rule adopted in a home is one of the following:

- The indoor area is totally smoke-free, with those wishing to smoke doing so outside.
- One room is designated as a place where people may smoke. Where possible, this room is one not used by children and infrequently used by those in the house who do not smoke. Ideally this is a room with a window and good ventilation to the outside. As no level has been shown to be safe when ETS exists, it is preferable to keep the level as low as possible.
- One room (or rooms) is designated as smoke-free; usually those used most frequently by people in the home who do not smoke and/or used rarely by visitors who want to smoke.
- Smoking may occur anywhere in the indoor area of the house.

Due to the small enclosed space in a vehicle like a car, there are only two choices — either smoking is allowed or it is not.

By making others aware of the rules for smoking in your home and car, those who smoke and those who do not know what to expect and there is less need for resentment on either part. One way to remind people of your rules is to provide signs which indicate them. Signs to indicate "no smoking" or "designated smoking areas" for homes are available from the offices of many of the national health organizations. Special signs for cars are also often available.

Verbal or written invitations can include information on household rules regarding smoking. For example, the bottom line of a written invitation could state: "This is a smoke-free event," "Smoking is allowed indoors," or "We have designated a separate room for smoking." This may seem unneccessary, bothersome or even impolite, but unless the rules are stated, particularly to those who are not already aware of them, resentment or other problems can cause unpleasantness at a gathering. It is helpful for people who smoke to know the rules ahead of time, especially if they will not be able to smoke indoors. It is helpful for people who do not smoke to know the rules ahead of time, especially if they will be exposed to ETS.

The tobacco issue is very controversial. Both those who smoke and those who do not will appreciate knowing the household rules, especially if they have never visited before, or if the rules have changed since they last visited. In this way, as a host or hostess you can make it easier for all of your guests to enjoy themselves.

Some individuals who do not want to have ETS in their home try to indicate it in a more subtle way, by removing all ashtrays from view and only supplying one when it is requested. When the ashtray is made available on request, many people who smoke will accept that as a signal that smoking is allowed. However, in this case, the person who supplied the ashtray may resent that the person who is now smoking did not pick up on the subtle cue of the absent ashtray. It is far better to give a more obvious indication of the rules regarding tobacco in the household, such as putting a sign on the door or letting the person know about the rules when the ashtray is requested. Otherwise, the person who smokes is presented with a mixed message. Inconsistent or unclear rules can lead to resentment on the part of one, or both, people involved.

Some parents do not want their children to smoke. One way to promote nonsmoking in your household is to make your home smoke-free. In some households a compromise may be needed for a period of time, when smoking is permitted only in one designated room which the children do not, or seldom, use. This room should not be seen as an "adults only" room, but one which has been designated for the use of those who have been unfortunate enough to become addicted to tobacco. If a room is designated, it should be made available to both adults and adolescents who smoke.

Promote Discussion About a Smoke-Free Rule

If you are planning to change your household rules regarding smoking, as with work-place policies, the new rules are more likely to be followed with fewer problems if all those affected by the change are made aware of it ahead of time. Close friends and relatives can be told of the change, for example, three months before the new rules comes into effect. Anyone visiting the home can then be made aware of, or reminded about, the new rules through the use of signs.

Figure 4. Three samples of smoke-free home signs. Courtesy of the Canadian Council on Smoking and Health and the British Columbia Lung Association.

When frequent visitors to your home know about the change ahead of time, they are given an opportunity to express their opinion and prepare their response. This advance discussion gives you an opportunity to explain to them the purpose of the change. If you are making your home smoke-free, you may want to use some of the following as discussion points:

• Your desire to eliminate environmental tobacco smoke from your home because of the health hazards related to it and the fact that no safe level has been determined.

• Your desire to indicate to your children and other young people that you are concerned about their health. Let frequent visitors know that you do not want your children to feel that you would approve of their smoking because you allow it in your home. Indicate that you feel that by allowing any smoking in your home you are indicating that you approve of it.

• That this rule is a reflection of your concern about environmental tobacco smoke and is not a reflection of your feelings toward any person. Let frequent visitors know that although you are eliminating tobacco smoke from your home, you welcome people who smoke as well as those who do not smoke, as long as they do not smoke in your home.

• That you appreciate the difficulty those addicted to tobacco have in not smoking for a long period of time and will understand if they need to go outdoors to smoke during their visits to your home. Where appropriate, you might indicate that they will probably have company outside as a number of friends or relatives smoke. This may be especially true during larger gatherings at your home. You might also consider offering to go outside with them while they smoke during their visit.

• If appropriate, you might indicate that you are aware that they have been trying to quit smoking and that you hope that this rule in your home will help them to do so. You might also like to offer other means of support to them as well. For example, you might be willing to have them phone you for support when they feel the urge to smoke or take them to lunch, a concert, a game, or another activity they enjoy as a reward for not smoking for a given period of time.

•If appropriate, let friends or relatives who are new exsmokers know that you hope this new rule in your home will help them remain nonsmokers. Indicate that you understand that many people begin smoking again because of pressure to smoke in social situations and you would not like this to happen to them in your home.

Avoid getting into a discussion of "rights" of smokers and nonsmokers as this makes it more of a personal issue and gets away from the fact that the purpose of a smoke-free rule is to eliminate exposure to ETS. Also, arguments that smoking is a legal act should be avoided, as the rules you set in your home are your own and you can narrow down legal activities to those which are acceptable to you in your own environment. One of the reasons that smoking is a legal act is that millions of North Americans are addicted to tobacco and it would cause major problems if the substance was made illegal.

You may be pleasantly surprised with the acceptance of a smoke-free rule in your home and car. Many people who smoke will appreciate knowing your feelings about environmental tobacco smoke and will comply with the rule. Those who smoke are becoming more and more aware of the problems of ETS and are making efforts not to expose others to it.

On the other hand, you will probably find that some of your friends and relatives will take the new rule as a personal affront and you will need to reassure them of your reasons for the new rule. Some will indicate an unwillingness to visit if your home is smoke-free. In this case you can assure them that they are welcome in your home even though they will have to smoke elsewhere. You might invite them to outdoor activities held at your home. You may also be willing to visit with them elsewhere where they can smoke and, if so, you can let them know this.

Creatively Dispose of Cues to Smoke

Once you have made your home and car smoke-free, you may have unused cigarettes, matches, lighters, and ashtrays still on hand. You will now need to decide what to do with them. You may decide to keep one ashtray for the use of people who smoke outside. Some matches could be saved to use for lighting candles when the power goes out, for lighting the fireplace, or for use when camping. Lighters may be used for similar purposes but fire safety must be kept in mind when using these for purposes other than those for which they were designed.

Ashtrays may be used as dishes for candy or nuts, plant pots or water catchers for plants, coasters, dishes for water or food for pets, or containers for odds and ends. You may decide to take them to a thrift sale or sell them at your garage sale. The ashtray in the car could be used to store keys, a card used to enter a locked parking area, dog biscuits to have handy on a trip with your pet, or change for parking, the laundromat, arcade games or copying machines.

Remaining cigarettes can be thrown out or given to a friend or relative, who does not smoke, to dispose of them. Since nicotine is a strong insecticide, you might try using it in the soil with your non-edible plants. This may not work as well with low tar and nicotine tobacco as it tends to contain more additives.

Be creative – think of your own ideas for disposing of, or finding alternate uses for, the equipment associated with smoking.

Chapter 5 : At Work

Anyone who wants a policy to restrict smoking in his or her work-place can benefit from the experiences of many other businesses and organizations which have already developed and implemented this kind of policy. In general, where a policy has included a well-planned marketing and communication strategy, the policy has been effective.

Ten Steps to a Work-place Policy

These steps can be used as a guide to develop a policy for your work-place. This guide can also be used to strengthen an existing policy if your work-place is not yet smoke-free, or if the present policy is not working.

Step 1: Gather Initial Information

Anyone in a business or organization can initiate this step by gathering information on smoking and the effects of environmental tobacco smoke from a variety of sources. The information could include specific information on your organization's experience with the tobacco smoke issue. More general information can also be included.

You may find information on the experience of other organizations with work-place policies, statistics on the estimated costs of work-place smoking to an employer, and the health effects of active smoking and exposure to ETS.

Background information on the experience of your organization may be accessible through your personnel or occupational health departments in a larger organization, or from the people responsible for these functions in a smaller organization. You are looking for reported ETS-related concerns from employees, makeshift policies that are occurring in some areas of the work-place because of these concerns, absenteeism of people who smoke or people who work in an area with ETS versus those who neither smoke nor work in an area with ETS, janitorial and maintenance costs related to tobacco smoke and smoking, and smoking-related medical and insurance costs.

By seeking this information, you may find that someone in your organization is already working on background information on a policy for the consideration of management. You may also find someone who is willing to work with you to put together a background paper. It is important that you have several friends or fellow employees who will work with you or support your efforts. You will find that some nonsmokers will not support your efforts, and some smokers will.

A good source of information about your own organization is your own observation. Estimate the number of nonsmokers where you work. What concerns have you heard expressed about the presence of ETS in your work-place by employees or by the public? Are there any special concerns? These may include the presence of pregnant employees whose unborn children may be adversely affected by ETS, or factors like poor ventilation or the production of other gases which increase the health risks related to ETS. When using your own observation as a basis for background material to give to management be as objective as possible in your presentation.

Information on general statistics on smoking and ETS related to the work-place, legal precedents and estimated costs of smoking to employers are usually available from your local public health department, or local or regional offices of national health organizations, such as the Heart Foundation, Cancer Society or Lung Association or a nonsmokers' rights association. These sources may also know of nonsmoking action groups in your area, and any organizations similar to yours which have policies that restrict smoking, or are in the process of developing this type of policy.

From these sources or city hall you can find out if there is a local ordinance in your municipality or a state/provincial law which restricts smoking in the work-place and how it affects your work-site. Your municipality may be in the process of developing an ordinance and you may wish to have some input on the inclusion of the work-place in its coverage.

National health organizations or public health sources may also be aware of any legal precedents or arbitration rulings in your state or province regarding ETS as a work-place health hazard. Find out from other work-places similar to your own how they went about implementing their policy, how effective they think their policy is, and what recommendations they would make to you for developing a policy. If there are no work-places in your community which have implemented the type of policy you would like in your work-place, find out about work-places in other communities with similar policies and the process they used and how effective they feel their policy is.

If there are existing nonsmoking action groups in your area, find out how they might assist you in your efforts. Some groups have a more radical approach to nonsmoking promotion and you may wish to take a more moderate approach to developing a policy where you work. However, these groups will often provide encouragement to you and can let you know about activities they are planning in your community which may be supportive of your efforts in your work-place.

Step 2: Obtain Management Support

Once you have gathered all your data, prepare a briefing note for management detailing why you feel a smoking policy should be implemented in your organization. The format of your presentation may be even more important than your data. Your efforts to this end will be in vain if no one reads your report or it is put aside for future reference. An ally in management is extremely useful at this point. Such a person can help you develop a report in a format which is most acceptable to top management in your organization, and may be willing to support your report at a management meeting. If you do not have an ally in management, find someone who does and who is also supportive of your efforts.

You may be asked to personally present a short verbal report or be available to answer questions at a management meeting. If so, it is very helpful to be briefed ahead of time as to who will be at the meeting, who will most likely support or not support your report and who will be the fence-sitters, and what points will be of most concern to them.

It is also helpful to know who has had an opportunity to read your report (some people may have been away from the office for several days or weeks), how much time you will have for your presentation (make sure to leave time for questions), and what else is on the agenda for the meeting (to judge where in importance the smoking issue will lie). In some cases, it may be wise to try to postpone your presentation until another meeting if it is to be sandwiched in between matters which will be considered of much higher priority by most of the management team.

It is important that top management is supportive of a work-place policy, as they will ultimately be responsible for its implementation and enforcement, and will need to be involved in any plans for education of employees and/or cessation programs or incentives. It is also very important for the success of the policy that all people in the organization adhere to it. If a manager smokes in a private office when this is not allowed for anyone else, there will be problems with compliance by a growing number of employees. If new people join management, check for their support.

The management people in your organization may not be willing at this point to implement a smoke-free policy, but they may be willing to have a survey of employees conducted to find out how many employees would like such a policy implemented, or who would like to see the present policy strengthened and, if so, how. They may also want to survey the public if the organization frequently has members of the public on the premises. The willingness of management to have a survey done should be considered encouraging even though they do not express support of a work-place policy at the present time. The results of the survey may well influence them to support a policy.

Step 3: Appoint a coordinator

One person must be designated by management to coordinate the processes of planning and implementing a policy. This person should have authority in the organization (be from senior or middle management) and have liaison with both management and staff. The delegated authority this person has should be clearly stated so that he or she can proceed with a minimal number of approvals from the full management team. If the organization is large, it may be useful to have assistance from the research department in order to develop, process and analyze the survey questionnaire results. Research staff can make sure that the questions are clear and precise and that the answers can be expected to be useful in future planning for the policy. This staff can also help to design a questionnaire format where the answers can be easily collated by computer.

It is essential that the coordinator support the development of a work-place policy to restrict smoking. The coordinator should also be willing to guide the development of the policy using a good knowledge base about smoking and ETS in relation to the work-place, skill in policy development in the organization, and a rational approach. He or she should acknowledge the importance of the health hazards related to ETS and the employee-relations problem caused by the annoyance factor of tobacco smoke. The coordinator should appreciate the concerns of employees who smoke as well as those who do not.

Step 4: Survey All Employees

A survey regarding tobacco smoke in the work-place must be made. This survey can be tailored to the needs of the organization, especially if it has more than one work-site, so that the concerns of employees in each work-site, or in each type of work-site, can be isolated for the purpose of designing a marketing and communication strategy for the policy.

Questions could cover the amount of restriction on smoking that the employees would like in their own work area as well as in breakrooms and other areas of the building. Fire regulations should be taken into account when giving options from which the employees can choose. For example, it may be against local fire regulations to smoke in a stairwell. Questions can also be asked about whether employees are bothered by tobacco smoke in the work-place, to what extent and in what way. Current smoking status should also be included.

The organization may also want to include questions regarding the level of support of company-offered incentives or cessation programs to employees (and perhaps family members) who smoke. Some organizations have used the questionnaire to gather information from employees on their ideas about a work-place health program which may include weight control, exercise, nutrition information, and other health-related topics, in addition to smoking cessation. Age category, sex, work-site location, full-time/part-time status, management/non-management status and the percentage of employees who smoke in the immediate work area are topics that have been included in some work-place questionnaires.

A very useful part of a questionnaire can be a "comments" section, where employees can express their opinions and ideas without being restricted by the question-answer format. This section is more difficult to collate but the results can be very worthwhile as it allows employees to air their feelings and gives the steering committee a better understanding of the employees' concerns related to tobacco and tobacco smoke.

The questionnaire should be written by individuals who are familiar with the goals of the survey and who are experienced in writing questionnaires that elicit accurate responses. Many organizations have used questionnaires as a basis for the development of their work-place policy and can give you advice on what questions they found useful and which ones should be rewritten or discarded. A collection of questionnaires can be used to develop one which is tailored to your organization. Examples of questionnaires that can be read by machine are available from some large organizations with work-place policies.

The method of distribution should ensure that every employee has an opportunity to complete and anonymously return a copy of the survey questionnaire. Your organization may want to ask employees who are interested in being involved in the development of a policy to contact their supervisor or the coordinator. This could give the coordinator a pool of names from which to form a steering committee.

The results of the survey should be compiled and shared with the participants and management.

Step 5: Appoint a Steering Committee

The coordinator now chooses the members for the steering committee. Members should include individuals from both non-management and management as well as people who smoke and those who do not. Where the workers are unionized, invitations can be extended for union representation on the committee. In organizations with more than one work-site, it is useful to have people representing different types of work-sites on the committee. The name of the committee should be positive, for example, "Clean Air" or "Nonsmoking promotion." A committee of eight to ten members is usually large enough to provide liaison with a variety of employee areas and small enough to be functional.The survey questionnaire, the newsletter of the organization, or another established communication mechanism within the organization can be used to find employees interested in being involved on the committee or promoting the policy in other ways. The coordinator needs to pick committee members who can work well together and will use a rational, thoughtful approach.

The purpose of the committee is usually to steer the development of the policy using the results of the survey, and it may also make recommendations to management on a marketing and communication strategy to implement the policy effectively. The committee may be involved in evaluation and follow-up after the policy comes into effect. The coordinator usually chairs the steering committee.

Step 6: Draft Policy and Recommend a Marketing and Communication Strategy

The steering committee uses the results of the survey as a basis to develop a draft of the policy and make recommendations for a planned approach to market the policy to all of the employees of the organization and to communicate the policy to all of those who will be affected by it.

The policy should be no more than one page in length and should state to whom it applies (employees, management, members of the public, staff from other organizations working at the work-place, anyone in the work-place), who is responsible for enforcing the policy, and when the policy will come into effect. The policy should specify where smoking will be allowed. This may include specific areas in each individual work-place, in some vehicles, and at meetings of the organization held outside the work-place. In large organizations, when the policy is to allow designated smoking areas but the many locations of work-places make it impractical to name specific rooms in each work-site, specific guidelines for the location of designated smoking areas and the type of room/space should be clearly identified.

The format of the policy can be the same as other personnel policies of the organization and, if so, should be included in the personnel manual. Noncompliance with the policy usually results in standard disciplinary procedures. Information on the consequences of noncompliance can be included in an employee memorandum containing questions and answers about the policy, if one is included in the communication plan.

In deciding when to implement a new policy, the rule of thumb in some areas has been that the period of time between the announcement of the policy and the date it comes into effect should be no less than three months. In some organizations, a six-month period is preferred, depending on the marketing and communication strategy being planned. When the organization decides on a two-step approach from "no policy" to a "smoke-free policy," an example of timing would be to introduce a designated-area policy within six months of the announcement of the policy and then, a year later, implement the totally smoke-free work-place policy where smoking is not allowed anywhere indoors in the work-place.

Depending on the questions used in the survey questionnaire and the responses received, the steering committee may now be in a position to make recommendations regarding cessation programs and incentives, health education programs, and other health-related incentives and programs for the organization.

These recommendations should include who within the organization will be responsible for the programs, how the programs will be implemented, the expected cost to the employee and the employer, how frequently they will be offered through the organization or in the community, how employees will find out about them, and to whom they will be offered.

These programs will be part of the marketing and communication strategy to improve the effectiveness of the policy. The steering committee may be involved in developing and making recommendations for this strategy. On the other hand, the coordinator may use comments previously obtained at committee meetings and from the employee survey to put together a planned strategy.

This strategy should include all four factors of the marketing mix:

• price (for example, savings to organization on janitorial services and fire insurance, savings on medical costs and health insurance premiums, cost of incentives or cessation programs);

- product (the policy);
- place (for example, promotional channels, like the organization's newsletter which are used to help sell the policy); and
- promotion (for example, incentives, "adopt a smoker" campaigns, news articles on work-place policies in other organizations and on smoking prevention programs in schools, cessation programs for employees and their family members, news releases about the policy, business cards to give to the public which state the organization's policy). The marketing mix should be planned according to the needs of the individual organization and its employees.

The communication plan is directly related to the marketing plan but its goal is to ensure that all those affected by the policy are aware of it before it comes into effect. If possible, they should also have some prior means of expressing their concerns about the policy. This is one reason for a three-month lag between the announcement of the policy and the date it comes into effect. One essential part of the communication plan is to ensure that all employees are made aware of the results of the survey. Your organization may also want to consider sending a memo to all employees, using a question-and-answer format which responds to commonly asked questions in the "comments" section of the survey questionnaire as well as questions related to compliance with the policy.

Communication with each employee can occur through such routes as payroll, organizational memoranda from top management or supervisors, meetings of the organization, or bulletin boards. It is important to provide for two-way communication so that employees can participate in the planning process and make the policy effective. The time taken now to communicate with employees may eliminate some future problems and encourage employees to be creative and positive in solving any future problems which do occur.

Signs are a way of providing an ongoing reminder of the policy. Along with press releases, these are especially useful to let members of the public know about the organization's new policy. Information on the types of signs to be used, where they are to be obtained, who will be responsible for their posting and ongoing maintenance, and where they will be posted (includ-

Figure 5. Two samples of smoke-free work-place signs. Courtesy of the Canadian Council on Smoking and Health.

ing in vehicles, where appropriate), needs to be included in the communication plan. Arrangements should be made to distribute the signs before the policy comes into effect. An example of clear signage would be to have a sign indicating that "This is a smoke-free building" or "Smoking is permitted only in designated areas" on each entrance to any building. Where areas for smoking have been designated, information on these could be made available at the front desk for visitors and in a newsletter and on bulletin boards for employees. International smoking signs (a picture of a cigarette with a green circle around it) could be used in designated smoking areas so that people become used to nonsmoking as the norm and smoke only in areas with signs.

The communication and marketing plans should be linked together to provide an overall strategy for effective implementation of the new policy. The timing of each stage should be mapped out to provide a comprehensive process over the months between the announcement of the policy and its implementation.

Step 7: Obtain Management Approval

At this point, the draft policy and the recommendations for incentives and programs, along with the marketing and communication strategy, are presented to management for approval. As with the briefing note on the initial background information, the format of this presentation is important. Again, make sure you address the points which will be of most concern to them. Briefly present the results of the survey and then the proposed policy. The extent of the information given to them on the marketing and communication strategy and incentives and programs will depend on the time available and the authority delegated to the coordinator. In other words, it depends on what approval the coordinator needs to proceed.

It may be necessary to revise the proposed policy depending on the response of management, or the coordinator may be given approval to proceed with the process. Because participation of individual members of the management team may be included in the promotion part of the marketing plan, or costs to the organization may be incurred in order to carry out the plans, it may be wise to check these expectations with the individuals most involved before the plan is presented to the entire management team.

Step 8: Implement Marketing and Communication Strategy

Once approval has been received from management, the strategy is implemented. During the months of this process, look for creative ideas presented by employees that may help to solve future problems and may improve the public relations image of the organization. The media can be helpful in promoting the policy, if used skillfully. Media reporters often look for polarization on the tobacco-smoke issue and may play up the smoker versus nonsmoker or rights issues if not given other angles with which to create a story.

Step 9. Implement Policy

The time between the beginning of Step 1 and Step 9 may be a year or longer. This may seem a long time to someone who is wanting to free their work-place of environmental tobacco smoke. Small organizations may be able to implement a policy at a much more rapid rate if there is a lot of support for such a policy and no major concerns exist on the part of any individuals. Also, the communication process can occur more quickly in a small organization.

By the time the policy comes into effect, all employees should be familiar with the policy and know who they can contact if they have concerns about it, where they can go for further information about cessation or educational programs, and where smoking is permitted. (This may include designated areas outside the building if the policy designates the work-place as smoke-free). In cases where members of the public use the work-place, mechanisms should be in place to make them familiar with the policy.

Those who will enforce the policy must be aware of this expectation and know how to carry out their role. They must also be aware of the importance of being consistent in their efforts to maintain compliance with the policy. Actions taken to deal with noncompliance may be more lenient during the first few months that the policy is in effect.

Step 10. Evaluate Effect of Policy and Implement Required Follow-up

The organization may wish to evaluate the effects of the policy, and this evaluation could be included in the marketing plan. This could include costs of absenteeism, maintenance of smoke-sensitive equipment, janitorial services before and after the policy came into effect, complaints and compliments received about the policy by employees and the public, and press coverage.

After six months or a year, it may be useful to survey the employees again, using questions similar to those in the original survey, to see if there are any changes in attitudes toward the policy, the percentage of nonsmokers in the organization, and the level of support for a more restrictive policy. Results of this survey may indicate a need to work on more consistent enforcement of the policy in some areas of the work-place, or a need to increase the restrictiveness of the policy.

Work-places Which Are Public Places

Some work-places, like recreation centers and shopping malls, are heavily used by the public. Where an ordinance or bylaw does not exist to cover these public places, some administrators have implemented a policy for their own facility, either for the office space only or for the entire facility. When introducing a policy for an entire facility, it may be useful to combine the steps used for work-place policy development and those used for ordinance/municipal bylaw development. For example, staff could be surveyed and in addition, a random sample of public users of the facility could be surveyed for their opinion of a new policy. The support of local politicians, key stakeholders and the media could be sought to increase public awareness of the policy and improve its effectiveness.

Communicating the policy to the public is extremely important when the facility is a public place. This communication should be positive in tone and may take various forms, including outdoor ashtrays at the entrances, highly visible signs with "no smoking" in both symbol and printed form at the entrances and throughout the building, notification of the policy on all brochures, flyers and other printed materials available to the public from the center, and articles in local newspapers regarding the introduction of the policy as well as progress reports over time.

A separate method is needed to communicate with staff members. For example, an internal newsletter or memorandum could be used for this purpose. Staff should be made aware of the policy well in advance and could be involved in developing the policy as well as enforcing it. They will need to receive training on how to deal with people who smoke in the facility, either fellow staff members or members of the public. The staff should also be given progress reports on the effectiveness of the policy and be encouraged to give ideas on how this could be improved. For example, the center may decide to offer cessation or prevention programs or campaigns to promote public awareness of the tobacco issue and promote the center's policy.

A Work-place Policy : One Company's Experience

The Insurance Corporation of British Columbia (ICBC) implemented a policy to restrict smoking on October 1, 1985. The company was a government-owned corporation with approximately 2400 employees. Half of the employees worked in the head office in North Vancouver in a building which had six floors and no co-tenant. The remainder of the employees worked in 40 to 50 claim centers located throughout the province of British Columbia. Each of these centers had between six and 70 employees. The following describes the process followed by this organization over the 18 months in which the policy was developed and implemented. The information was obtained from Herb Mills, manager of employee relations at ICBC and from Shirley Thompson, smoking and health consultant, British Columbia Lung Association.

Step 1: Gather Initial Information (May - October 1984)

In May 1984, the vice-president of administration asked the manager of employees relations, Herb Mills, to attend a work-place policy seminar presented by the American Lung Association in Tacoma, Washington. The impetus behind this request was a growing number of complaints by employees about environmental tobacco smoke and the fact that physicians' reports were indicating that ETS was a contributing cause of some employee absenteeism. In addition, makeshift policies were being implemented in some areas of the work-place because of the nuisance factor of ETS.

After returning from the seminar, Mills began to gather background information for a report to management which would identify the issues and reasons why the organization should develop its own policy. This included the problems documented by the company regarding employee absenteeism, employee complaints and makeshift policies. These policies included the existence of separate times for use of the cafeteria by smokers and nonsmokers and the fact that employees were putting up physical barriers in their work areas to try to decrease their exposure to ETS. Mills also collected information on medical, legal and economic reasons for a policy and examples of how other companies and municipalities were responding to the issue. At the time, there was no other large organization in the area which had an extensive policy that restricted smoking.

In order to estimate the costs to ICBC related to smoking, Mills used general information on absenteeism, accident and productivity rates for those who smoke versus those who do not, lost earnings due to illness and death, maintenance and property-damage costs, costs of air-purifying equipment and costs due to exposure to ETS. This data was then applied to ICBC using the number of employees and offices, absenteeism rates, estimated percentage of employees who smoke, average salary of employees, company contributions to health, disability, and life insurance plans, taxes paid for pension plan, hospital programs, and unemployment insurance programs, and janitorial costs. The resulting estimate of annual costs to the corporation due to allowing smoking and ETS in the workplace are indicated in Table 3.

Step 2. Obtain Management Support (November-December 1984)

Mills presented his report to the executive group of the organization and obtained approval from them to proceed with the development and implementation of a policy.

Step 3. Appoint a Coordinator (December 1984)

Mills was given this leadership role at ICBC because it was felt that the issue of ETS was an employee-relations concern. It was felt that leadership should come from the area in the organization dealing with personnel policy, not from an area dealing with health. However, occupational health staff were involved in providing background information and the corporation used the consultative services available from the British Columbia Lung Association. Mills set a minimum goal of assigning smoking to designated areas only because he felt

Table 3

Costs to ICBC Each Year for Allowing Smoking in the Work-place, per Employee Who Smokes

Cause	Cost (dollars)
Absenteeism	330
Medical Care	230
Illness and Early Death	385
Insurance (excluding Health)	68
On-the-Job Time Lost	1716
Property Damage and Depreciation	500
Maintenance	53
Air Cleaning/Purifying Equipment	64
Nonsmokers' Exposure to ETS	500
Total Cost per Smoker per Year	$3,846
Total Annual Cost to ICBC	$3,846,000

Source: **Smoking in the Work-place: Policy and Procedures Manual,** British Columbia Lung Association, October, 1986.

any lesser step would not provide an effective health-related policy.

On February 20, 1985, a staff memo signed by the vice-president of administration went out to every employee in the organization. The memo outlined the growing concerns regarding the hazards of environmental tobacco smoke and the benefits of a smoke-free work-place. It concluded by stating, "It is essential that this corporation plan, develop and adopt a policy which identifies smoke, not smokers or smoking, as the issue." Comments on this memo were invited through an internal newsletter and about a dozen employees responded and expressed support and interest.

Step 4: Survey All Employees (March 1985)

The survey questionnaire included questions related to whether or not the employees felt there was a need for a policy, how restrictive they felt a policy should be, the extent that smoke bothered them in the work-place, how ETS affected the employees, and employee smoking status. The survey responses were separated according to whether they were received from the head office or from claim centers. Some of the questions were to be answered only by those employees who were current smokers. The survey also invited comments at the bottom of the form.

Of the 2200 survey forms sent out, 1600 were returned. Of these, 80 percent indicated support for management to implement a policy. This included 50 percent of employees who smoked. This may have been because some employees who smoked were tired of being hassled about where they could or could not smoke. The written comments gave those who felt strongly about the issue an opportunity to state their opinions and some people wrote pages.

Step 5: Appoint a Steering Committee (April 1985)

The timing of the formation of the committee was such that the members first met at a workshop called "Smoking Policies in the Work-place" sponsored by the British Columbia Lung Association. The eight people on the committee were chosen by Mills for their ability to think logically and look at the issue rationally. Five were nonsmokers and three were smokers; four members were from claim centers and four were from the head office. Mills was the only person from management involved with the committee and he played a low-key role. The committee was called the "Corporate Smoking Policy Committee" and all correspondence went out under this name. Mills did not want the policy to be seen as one which was management-engineered .

Each committee member was given 200 returned survey forms so that they could read the narrative comments and determine any trends. One typical response was, "Be quick, I'm expiring." Of those responding, 40 percent of the employees indicated that they were always or frequently bothered by smoke in the work-place. This indicated how much of an employee-relations problem it was. One-third of the employees were exsmokers, one-third currently smoked and one-third had never smoked. There was a difference in smoking status between the head office where 47 percent had never smoked, and the claim centers where 35 percent had never smoked.

It was felt that the smoking policy was an employee-relations issue which should be handled by management, but union representatives were invited to the committee meetings and minutes were sent to them. The union did not send a representative to the committee meetings but six months after the policy was implemented, the union issued its own policy. This endorsed the corporation's policy but indicated that the union could not condone disciplinary action for violation of the corporation's policy.

Step 6: Draft Policy and Recommend a Marketing and Communication Strategy (April - June 1985)

Mills developed a marketing and communication strategy and its implementation began in February 1985 when all employees were made aware, through a memorandum, that the corporation was planning to develop a policy. Contents of this strategy are outline in Step 8.

In May and June 1985, the Smoking Policy Committee met five times to work on the policy, and in June the proposed policy was presented to the executive.

Step 7: Obtain Management Approval (June 1985)

The policy received approval from the executive when it was presented in June. The president of the corporation, who was a chain-smoker, supported the policy and agreed to comply with it. The results of the employee survey undoubtedly had an impact on his decision. All of the committee members also endorsed the policy. Of the three people on the committee who smoked, two attempted to quit smoking and the other agreed that something should be done, and understood the rationale behind the policy, but did not personally want to quit smoking.

The proposed policy, sent out to employees in July, indicated that although the goal was to eventually make all of the buildings smoke-free, as of October 1, 1985 smoking would be allowed only in designated areas. In the head office, these would consist of one of the two small coffee rooms on each of the six floors and in half of the cafeteria. In each of the claim centers, the lunch room would be the designated smoking area.

Step 8: Implement Marketing and Communication Strategy (February - October 1985)

The proposed policy, distributed to all employees by early July 1985, had a tentative implementation date of October 1, 1985. Accompanying the policy was a memo asking for comments, and a list of 23 questions and answers related to the comments received in response to the survey. These questions and answers were useful in responding to the concerns of employees and reducing their doubts about the effectiveness of the policy. A copy of the contents of this memo to the staff is found in Appendix B.

In response to the proposed policy, less than a dozen letters were received by the Corporate Smoking Policy Committee. The letters were received from employees who either felt that the policy did not go far enough, or were concerned about how the policy would affect members of the public who came to the claim centers. As the responses to the draft did not necessitate rewriting any of the policy, the draft became the actual policy.

Information on the issue of environmental tobacco smoke was supplied to the employees in various forms. Five articles were written for issues of the corporation's newsletter from March to June on subjects such as the growing popularity of smoke-free air and what was happening in work-places and cities in various parts of the country. A videotape on the effects of environmental tobacco smoke was shown to employees. The Canadian Cancer Society's cartoon booklet, "Second Hand Smoke", was put on each employee's desk.

Figure 6. "No Puffin" symbol developed by the Insurance Corporation of British Columbia to communicate the Clean Air policy to staff and the public in a lighthearted manner. Courtesy of Insurance Corporation of British Columbia.

There was a need to provide a support system for those who wanted to quit smoking. The only program that was available throughout the province was one offered by the Seventh Day Adventists. Thirty-six employees took advantage of this program, which was offered to groups of employees after work. The corporation sponsored these groups for a cost to the employer of $20 per employee. Other employees were given the option of using other cessation programs and the corporation would reimburse them for costs incurred up to $20, in return for their receipt. There was no proof required to substantiate that they had quit smoking. Some "Freedom from Smoking" manuals from the B.C. Lung Association were also purchased. The total cost to the corporation for cessation programs was between $1000 and $2000.

In the head office, the cafeteria and coffee areas were provided with exhaust fans and ventilated to the outside. In the smaller buildings, the use of the lunch room for the designated smoking area was the best interim solution but many of these rooms were not on the outside of the building so the smoke would quickly fill the room. Some filtration equipment was installed in the ceilings to eliminate some of the particulate portion of the smoke but the gas portion was still present. Employees were therefore still exposed to the hazardous substances found in ETS.

Step 9: Implement Policy (October 1, 1985)

Because ICBC was the first large organization in British Columbia to implement a policy to this extent, they received a fair amount of press attention. In order to remind employees about the imminent policy, press releases were sent out to employees and the press at the same time four to five days in advance of the October 1 implementation date. On September 12, the president sent out a memo to the managers of the organization reminding them of the policy and the reasons for it.

The corporation wanted to give the message to the public in a light-hearted way and used the "No Puffin" sign for this purpose. This sign consisted of the figure of a bird, the puffin, with the slogan "No Puffin, Our Policy is Clean Air". These signs were made available in a "tent" card format to all offices. An eight-foot styrofoam figure of "No Puffin" was moved to various locations in the head office during October and a

ICBC'S CLEAN AIR

We are striving for an environment which contributes to the health and comfort of everyone in the building.

Please refrain from smoking.

Figure 7. Information card developed by the Insurance Corporation of British Columbia to give to members of the public who were smoking in a smoke-free space on the company's premises. Courtesy of the Insurance Corporation of British Columbia.

picture of the figure with the president of the corporation was featured in an article in the corporation's newsletter.

A decal outlining the "clean air" policy was posted on the outside doors of the offices, and this information was also made available in a business-card format for employees to give to members of the public who were smoking in the building. In most cases, when approached in a polite, non-authoritarian way, members of the public complied with the policy.

Step 10: Evaluate Effect of Policy and Implement Required Follow-up

Six months after the policy came into effect, an article in the corporation's newsletter reviewed policy progress and let employees know about the attention the corporation had received. This included over 100 inquiries from around the province and outside of British Columbia about the implementation of a work-place policy and the fact that Mills had made various presentations at work-place policy seminars across Canada. This article in the corporation's newsletter commended the employees for their leadership role.

The timing for the next step — to a smoke-free policy — has now been determined. The designated-area policy was successfully implemented, but there was still concern about exposure to ETS, especially in the lunch rooms of the claim centers. Another employee survey was conducted in the fall of 1987 and a report on the results and recommendations for future actions was submitted to the executive of the corporation in early 1988. This report has received executive endorsement and all offices will be smoke-free on August 2, 1988.

Smoke-Free Policies for Hospitals : One Hospital's Experience

A hospital presents a special case for a smoke-free policy. Although it is a work-place, it is also a short- or long-term, residence for individuals who are not employees. Many of the people who become patients in the hospital do so partly because of an addiction to tobacco.

There is a growing demand for hospitals to have smoke-free policies to provide a healthy environment for both staff and patients. On the other hand, there is the problem of patients who are addicted to tobacco. They may be trying to deal with severe mental or physical illness, and may find it difficult to cope with withdrawal from tobacco at the same time.

In Swedish Hospital Medical Center in Seattle, a regional referral center, a smoke-free policy was introduced over a two-year period. Ray Zoellick, associate executive director, was chairman of the Smoking Policy Committee and he provided the following information on their policy. It was decided that each time a new policy was introduced, information about the pending change would be made available two months before the effective date to all employees of the hospital and to the medical staff. Those affected by the policy could then discuss their thoughts and feelings about it, and, if they wished, make their comments known to either Zoellick, or Allan W. Lobb, M.D., chief executive officer of the hospital, before the policy came into effect.

In 1984, a policy was introduced which allowed smoking only in designated areas. The areas designated at that time were the employee lounge areas and part of the cafeteria. It was up to each unit to decide whether or not to designate their lounge area for smoking. This policy, which allowed for variations on the units, was a problem for some patient areas. The nursing staff requested the introduction of a comprehensive policy in which individual areas were not responsible for deciding whether or not a smoking area would be designated on their unit.

One year later, in 1985, the hospital policy was changed to allow smoking only in individual patient rooms. After complaints by some staff, it was changed to also allow smoking in one separate area of the cafeteria. This separate room became very congested with smoke. More ventilation was introduced into the area. The air filters for this small area in the cafeteria had to be changed at least twice a week. The walls also had to be washed regularly as they became discolored with the smoke. This provided a clear reminder of the pollution caused by the tobacco smoke.

By 1986, the medical and administrative staff in the hospital decided there was a need to take a stronger stand on the issue of smoking in the hospital. As a result, the committee worked on a smoke-free policy which came into effect in September 1986. With this policy, which is currently in effect, the hospital is smoke-free with a few minor exceptions. Because this final change in the policy meant that patients were no longer allowed to smoke in the hospital, there was a need to inform the public of the policy. This was done by sending "tent" cards with information about the policy to all the active medical staff to use in their offices. Also, all patients who were coming to the hospital on a non-emergency basis received details of the policy with their pre-registration information. They were also informed of the policy verbally on admission. All patient brochures on hospital services now include information on the smoke-free policy. The hospital is also well-signed throughout, and has a sign at the entrance which states: "This is a nonsmoking hospital. We care about your health and safety."

The hospital has held cessation programs for staff members and has made a chewing gum containing nicotine available to some staff members. The hospital now hires only nonsmokers.

It was decided that the nursing staff should not be required to enforce the smoke-free policy. If a patient persists in smoking, the problem is referred to the patient's physician who then makes the decision as to whether or not the patient will be allowed to smoke. If so, the physician writes an order to allow this. This situation only exists in exceptional circumstances and can only occur in a private room. For example, some patients being treated for cancer have been permitted to smoke in their own rooms. Even with the efficient hospital ventilation system, when smoking does occur in a private room, some tobacco smoke escapes into the hallways. The hospital has had some complaints about this but, at this time, allowing some patients to smoke in exceptional circumstances is felt to be a compassionate compromise. In spite of these few exceptions, Swedish Hospital essentially provides a smoke-free environment for staff, visitors, and patients.

This enforcement policy at Swedish Hospital is similar to that of other hospitals which have become smoke-free. Although no staff or visitors are allowed to smoke, in some exceptional circumstances, some patients who are long-term residents, mentally ill, or in palliative care, are permitted to smoke with their physician's consent.

Some hospitals have been concerned that smoke-free policies will result in staff or patients going elsewhere. In some cases where this was seen as a potential problem, hospitals in the area have worked together to institute a new policy on the same date. This eliminates the "competitive" aspect of smoking policies.

More and more hospitals are becoming role models for providing a smoke-free environment. Find out about the current policy in your local hospital(s), and ask what plans are being made to introduce a smoke-free policy, if one is not already in effect.

Chapter 6 : Etiquette and Nonsmoking

We are living in an interesting period in the evolution of social practices related to the behavior of smoking. After the Second World War, smoking reached a very high level of social acceptance by all ages and both sexes. The result was that many people smoked, and these individuals – adults and adolescents alike – pressured their peers to smoke too.

The use of tobacco was integrated into our society. A look at the social norms of the past decades indicates just how integrated it became. Hosts and hostesses were expected to have cigarettes available for their guests. Ashtrays were manufactured as part of fine china sets and were used as popular gift items. Smoking implements such as cigarette lighters and cigarette containers were also used as gifts. Every home was expected to have one or more ashtrays, even if no one who lived there smoked tobacco. Ashtrays were also provided on every table in restaurants, at meetings, and in public places.

Ashtrays became part of the design of cars and other transportation vehicles like buses, trains and airplanes. Cigarettes and other tobacco products were widely advertised in print media, on billboards, and on corner stores. Clocks in retail outlets, bus shelters, public benches, and items associated with sports and cultural events – from racing cars to theatre programs – were all used to advertise tobacco products.

Matches were given out free to customers of hotels, motels and restaurants. Cigarettes and other tobacco products became accessible for purchase 24 hours a day and were found in easy-to-access outlets like service stations and vending machines. This ease of availability was extended to young people even though in Canada it is against the law to sell tobacco products to those under 16 years of age. Most states in the United States also restrict selling of tobacco to minors, which in the majority of states is defined as those under 18 years of age. The social norm of smoking tobacco was, therefore, reinforced and cues to smoke (such as availability of ashtrays, matches and cigarettes), helped to promote the habit.

This previous promotion of smoking as a social norm has led to today's unusual circumstances. While we now have a wealth of information on the health hazards of active smoking and a growing knowledge of the health hazards related to exposure to environmental tobacco smoke, we also have millions of North Americans addicted to tobacco. This leads to a potentially difficult situation where people who do not smoke may feel forced to choose between their health (and that of their families) and the friendship and goodwill of their relatives and friends who are addicted to tobacco.

Determining the Rules

In your own personal environment, you can determine your own rules for smoking. Outside your own personal environment, the rules of society, or etiquette, take over where there is no established policy; for example in the work-place or public places. It is important to be aware of how a work-place policy, ordinance or bylaw, or state/provincial law affects you personally. Check with your employer, municipal staff or state/provincial government to find out what regulations and laws exist and how they affect you.

In the case of municipal or state/provincial regulations, local health authorities and organizations may also be able to give you information. Knowing the regulations is especially important for those people who smoke, as they may find they are unknowingly breaking the law. This may be especially true in municipalities where the ordinance or bylaw has specified that the norm is nonsmoking. In these cases smoking may only occur in designated smoking areas. All other indoor areas are to be kept free of environmental tobacco smoke.

In areas without policies or legislation, the rules are determined by etiquette, or what is considered correct social behavior. One of the reasons for many policies or legislative acts regarding smoking in the past few years is that the rules of social behavior have become very confusing. This is particularly true since the public has become aware of the evidence of the health effects of exposure to ETS. The result has been makeshift policies based on individual preferences and a lot of upset people who want to either eliminate tobacco smoke from their environment or smoke in peace. As in homes, there is a need for a clearing of the air over this issue and an establishment of policies and regulations in all workplaces and public places. Information on how to go about initiating this type of activity is found in other chapters of this book.

Until policies and regulations do exist, you may find the following guidelines useful:

• If you are a person who smokes, you should, before lighting up, ask those around you whether they mind if you smoke. If you are asked this question and you do mind, it is not impolite to say "Yes, I do mind." In fact, it is more polite to say this than to indicate that you really do mind by gestures, facial expressions or verbal statements after the person has begun to smoke.

• If you smoke, remember that it is impolite to smoke in a confined space such as an elevator.

• In a dining situation where smoking is allowed, try to plan seating arrangements so that those who wish to smoke are seated together.

• Tobacco smoke affects the senses of taste and smell. If you smoke, do not light up while others are eating, especially in very small restaurants.

• If you smoke, you should purchase and supply your own cigarettes.

• Always extinguish cigarette butts before discarded them. All butts should be placed in an ashtray, flushed down a toilet, or thrown into a lit fire (except for filter-tipped cigarettes which may be fire-proof and will not burn). Matches and ashes should be discarded in a similar manner.

Filter-tipped cigarettes may not decompose and may remain indefinitely if tossed onto the ground. For this reason, a receptacle for butts should be provided outside those homes which are smoke-free and where visitors who smoke do so outdoors.

If you smoke, you may wish to carry a covered ashtray with you so that you will always have a receptacle for used butts. A self-supplied ashtray should never be used indoors where smoking is not permitted. Any butt which is discarded when still lit can cause damage and fire if it falls near any combustible material. Butts are unattractive and smell, and should be disposed of as soon as possible. People who smoke should offer to clean the ashtray they have used, if one is supplied, when visiting a private home where the hosts do not smoke.

• Persons who smoke should only do so in a designated smoking area or with permission of those around them in an area where no regulations exist regarding smoking and where smoking is considered the norm. Similarly people who do not smoke should not use a designated smoking area and then complain about the smoke if they have the option to use an area where smoking is not permitted.

• Persons who do not smoke and who do not want to be exposed to environmental tobacco smoke should implement a smoke-free rule in their homes. They should also work toward smoke-free policies in their work-places and public places, where these do not exist, so that ETS is eliminated from their environment.

In homes where people who smoke and people who do not smoke live together, it will be necessary to come to an agreement on the rules for the household concerning smoking. In some cases the easiest solution is to designate a room for smoking. This should be one that is rarely or never used by children and that has ventilation to the outside.

• For those people who smoke, in order not to offend or to break the law, it is best to assume that any indoor area is considered nonsmoking unless you inquire and find out otherwise. This includes the common area of shopping malls which are included in some municipal regulations.

Figure 8. Postage stamp sold in Japan at the time of the Sixth World Conference on Smoking and Health held in Tokyo in November 1987.

CLEARING THE AIR THROUGH LEGISLATION

"The Smoke Ring is the ring of political and economic interests which has protected the tobacco industry for the past twenty years... The clear lesson...is that the Smoke Ring can only be broken if governments detach themselves from it. Consumers cannot do it alone. To do so requires an act of rare political courage."
Taylor, Peter. **Smoke Ring — The Politics of Tobacco**. Bodley Head Ltd.: London, 1984. pp. xix and 281.

Figure 9. Tent card developed for use in promoting the City of Vancouver bylaw. Courtesy of the British Columbia Lung Association.

Chapter 7 : Promoting Ordinances and Bylaws

During the past five years, the rate at which new ordinances and bylaws which restrict smoking have been passed in cities, municipalities, counties and regional districts across North America has been increasing rapidly. New and updated ordinances and bylaws are becoming more restrictive as to where smoking is permitted.

Ten Steps to an Ordinance/Bylaw

These steps, similar to those used in developing a work-place policy, can be used as a guide to promote an ordinance or bylaw. They are outlined in the following section on the experiences of Vancouver, British Columbia.

A Municipal Bylaw : One City's Experience

During 1986, Vancouver, British Columbia, a city with a population of approximately 430,000, celebrated its centennial and hosted Expo '86. This same year, the city council passed a bylaw which dealt with second-hand and sidestream smoke in buildings open to the public and in the work-place.

This was the first bylaw in Canada to regulate smoking in the work-place. What follows is a description of how this bylaw came about and how it was received. This information was obtained through an interview with Geoff Rowlands, unit director, Vancouver City Health Department and from Graham Cobb, the Health Department's bylaw enforcement coordinator.

Step 1: Gather Initial Information

A community health survey had been done in Vancouver in 1982-83 by a market research company. This survey included questions about smoking status and the level of public support for restrictions on smoking in a variety of public places and the work-place. From the 1700 household questionnaires completed, 630 demographically representative households were selected for analysis. This survey indicated that 74 percent of the adults living in Vancouver were nonsmokers or exsmokers. Table 4 shows the percentages of Vancouverites who indicated that they would support a ban or other restrictions on smoking in various locations, according to the results of the survey. The percentages of responses received from those who smoked are given separately in the second column.

Of those who supported restrictions on smoking, approximately one-third supported a complete ban of smoking in indoor areas and two-thirds supported designated smoking areas.

Step 2: Get On the Political Agenda

As a result of various incidents in the city, the issue was placed on the political agenda.

A nonsmoking promotion activists group, Airspace, was formed in 1985 and was vocal in the media about the need for smoking restrictions. The media publicized several workplace incidents including one where a secretary had to leave her job because of health problems related to environmental tobacco smoke – her employers were unwilling to help her eliminate ETS from her work environment.

By early 1985, more research information on the health effects of environmental tobacco smoke was being made available. At this time, a member of the public, a freelance legal secretary whose parents had both died of lung cancer associated with active smoking, became concerned about the problem of ETS. With the assistance of representatives of Airspace and the British Columbia Lung Association, as well as a labor

Table 4

Percentage of Vancouverites Who Would Support a Ban or Other Restrictions on Smoking in Various Locations, Community Survey 1982-83

Location	All	Smokers
Restaurants	92%	89%
Food Stores	93	91
Public Buildings	79	78
Public Transport	95	95
Health Facilities	86	95
Community Centers	86	86
Work-places	76	54

Source:Rowlands, G.D. **The Strategy Planning and Marketing Processes Behind the First Work-place Smoking Bylaw in Canada.** Paper presented to the British Columbia Public Health Association, May 1987.

lawyer, she wrote a report on the problems associated with ETS and sent it to the mayor of Vancouver, requesting that the city council regulate smoking in all public buildings in the city.

Step 3: Appoint a Civic Employee to Coordinate Planning and Implementation

This letter and report were referred from the mayor to the city medical health officer who in turn gave it to one of the health unit directors. This manager, Geoff Rowlands, had previously been interested in developing a work-place policy for all civic workers as well as a municipal bylaw to restrict smoking in public places. This letter and report from a member of the public helped to put the issue on the city's active political agenda and Rowlands was given the authority to prepare a draft bylaw for the city. He was also asked to draft a work-place policy for civic workers, as the city did not at that time have any restrictions on smoking for the areas in which its own staff worked.

Step 4: Gather Further Information, and Survey Civic Employees If No Civic Work-place Policy Is In Effect

Rowlands collected samples of ordinances and bylaws from municipalities across Canada and the United States. This included a summary of all bylaws in Canada produced annually by the Calgary City Health Department. He also reviewed the available epidemiological information on ETS and did a thorough analysis of the results of the 1982-83 market research study on community health in the city.

By early 1985, only a few municipalities in the province of British Columbia had bylaws restricting smoking in public places. It appeared that municipal bylaws could be effective through use of signs, publicity and public awareness, and public support.

Toronto, Ontario, another large Canadian city, had passed a bylaw seven years before. Several other cities across Canada also had existing bylaws which covered public places. None of the existing bylaws in Canada included restrictions in the work-place.

Two laws in the United States, one in San Francisco and one in Minnesota, were identified as examples which most closely represented Rowland's goals for a bylaw in Vancouver. In addition, he wanted it clearly understood that nonsmoking was the norm and that people in Vancouver could expect protection from exposure to environmental tobacco smoke in public places and in their work-place.

By 1985, there was growing evidence about the health consequences of exposure to ETS. In particular, information was available on the increased risk of lung cancer in spouses of people who smoked. There was also an increasing number of cases in the United States and Canada, where employees were taking grievances regarding unsafe exposure to ETS in the work-place either to arbitration or to court, using the argument that ETS is a hazardous substance.

A review of the results of Vancouver's 1982-83 marketing survey again confirmed that city residents would be very supportive of a bylaw to restrict smoking, not only in public places, but also in work-places. This information was useful as background data to gain support for the bylaw from local politicians.

It was essential that the city be prepared to introduce a work-place policy for civic employees in conjunction with a bylaw which would require smoking restrictions in the work-place. It was also important for civic employees to have, in advance, an opportunity to say what they thought the civic policy should be. As a result, a survey was held in May 1985 to obtain information and opinions from the civic employees.

By December 1985, the results of the survey were available and they closely resembled the results of the market survey of the public held a few years previously. This meant that the civic employees were also supportive of a work-place policy which restricted smoking and would support a municipal bylaw which included this.

Step 5: Write Draft of Bylaw

Using the information he had obtained from studying existing laws, ordinances, and bylaws from across North America, Rowlands wrote a draft of the bylaw for the City of Vancouver. One of the lawyers from the city's legal department, Brian Porter, worked on the legal framework for the bylaw and recommended that the smoking provisions be in the form of an amendment to the Vancouver City Health Bylaw. This resulting draft was then reviewed with the medical health officer and prepared for presentation to city council.

Step 6: Identify Key Stakeholders and Develop a Marketing Strategy to Reach Them

The next step was to identify the key stakeholders (those who would have the greatest potential influence and/or interest in the bylaw). These individuals and organizations were then separated into three groups: those who would most likely be supportive of the bylaw, those who would most likely be against the bylaw, and those whose position was not known or predictable. Those "for" and "against" were rated for their level of potential influence. Using this process, 280 key stakeholders were identified and most were considered to be supportive.

Those judged to be "for" the bylaw were organizations with some interest in health and safety, business and employers' organizations, some trade unions, and a variety of non-profit associations. Those judged to be against the bylaw included tobacco store owners and tobacco manufacturers. Those whose position could not be predicted included civil liberties organizations and some trade unions.

It was felt that the mayor was supportive of the bylaw but after individual meetings with some of the other 10 council members, it was still unclear how they would vote. Five of the council members smoked and six did not. One of the aldermen was also the executive director of the British Columbia Hotel and Restaurant Association. He preferred that the smoking policy in restaurants be left to voluntary compliance, rather than be included in the bylaw.

Step 7: Plan and Implement Marketing Strategy to Obtain Political Approval

Marketing focused on the use of the media to promote a positive message, strategically-timed information-sharing with key stakeholders, direct and indirect promotion to members of the city council, and promotion through information-sharing with targeted members of the public.

• Media

The city health department had a list of key media people who would be interested in the issue of nonsmoking and the bylaw. Through these contacts, news stories and radio and television interviews were released. The messages given focused on the overwhelming public support for a bylaw and the importance of the need for the nonsmoking majority to be heard. This use of the media allowed the health department to emphasize the positive aspects of a bylaw.

Whenever a new issue related to smoking was covered in the news (for example, airline regulations banning smoking, arbitration cases related to work-place and exposure to ETS), comment on the issue or follow-up stories were provided through the city health department to increase local coverage of the issue. Public support for a bylaw in Vancouver was always emphasized in these comments and stories.

• Key Stakeholders

Before the city council was asked for its support in proceeding with a bylaw, information was distributed to key stakeholders. Those judged to be in favor of the bylaw were sent a letter informing them of the health department's intention to introduce a bylaw which would restrict smoking in public places and work-places. They were also sent a press release which summarized the health consequences of exposure to ETS and a request that they contact members of the city council to let them know what they thought of the proposed bylaw.

Those judged to be against the bylaw were sent a copy of the press release regarding the proposed bylaw at the same time that it was sent to the media.

Those key stakeholders whose position could not be predicted were sent letters about the bylaw prior to the council meeting but they were not asked to take any action. In addition, the issue of civil liberties was addressed by the health department in local newspaper articles.

The use of this strategy for the key stakeholders was an attempt to capitalize on the support of those "for" a bylaw, to neutralize those "against," and to change the "fence-sitters" into supporters. Many of the stakeholders judged to be "for" a bylaw, did write or telephone members of the city council expressing their support. This occurred just before the issue was brought before the council.

The tobacco manufacturers kept track of the Vancouver bylaw situation through a firm of lawyers in Nova Scotia which obtained copies of all the relevant council reports and supporting documents. The tobacco store owners were not concerned about a bylaw as long as the public could smoke in their stores.

• Approval from City Council

At this point, the first report on a bylaw to restrict smoking was given to the city council. In his report, the medical health officer indicated his intent to produce a bylaw which would include public places and work-places. The report included the results of the work-place survey of the civic employees and the fact that Vancouver was already well behind Toronto, which had had a bylaw restricting smoking for seven years. In view of the results of the market research, positive press coverage, and the support given by local organizations, council gave unanimous approval to go ahead with formulating a bylaw.

The number of stories and comments given to the media increased from this point until an outline of the proposed bylaw was taken to the council.

The second report to the city council included information obtained from the review of bylaws across the United States and Canada. It also emphasized the importance of making the behavioral norm of nonsmoking also the accepted social norm. It was pointed out that under the Vancouver Charter, a provincial statute which delegates a set of responsibilities from the provincial government to the city council of Vancouver, the council had the responsibility to protect the health of the people of Vancouver. After this second report was given, the city council gave unanimous approval in principle to the outline of the proposed bylaw. The lawyer and unit director then worked cooperatively to put together the final wording of the draft legislation.

Again the media coverage was intensified during the weeks before the bylaw was taken to the city council for final approval. Several lobbying groups addressed the council at the meeting when the final report was presented to the council. Presentations were made by a local nonsmokers' rights group, the provincial branch of the Lung Association, the provincial medical association, and a smokers' rights advocate.

At this council meeting in May 1986, the bylaw was unanimously approved by the city council. The regulations concerning public places would come into effect on June 9, 1986 and the regulations for work-places would become effective on December 1, 1986 in order to allow businesses more time to work on their own policies.

Step 8. Market Bylaw to the Public

The target of the marketing of the bylaw now turned toward key members of the public – businesses and business organizations and people who did not smoke.

Part of the strategy of making nonsmoking the social norm was to have signs for smoking areas, rather than signs for nonsmoking areas. This meant that people who smoke had to find a place to do so, rather than people who do not smoke looking for a designated area for clean air.

This idea was promoted through a news release, articles in the newspapers and stories on radio and television. A pamphlet explaining the reasons for the bylaw and its contents was distributed to the public through city hall, the health department, the Lung Association, libraries, community centers, the Board of Trade and other organizations. This pamphlet was available on request to individuals or community groups.

Twenty-two thousand Vancouver businesses were identified and during the summer of 1986, each received, from the health department, a copy of the pamphlet which contained the new bylaw regulations.

A local company which sold air cleaning and ventilation equipment prepared its own pamphlet about the bylaw and advertised signs which they sold to businesses. These signs, approved by the health department, included international symbols. Those for entrances to buildings said, "No smoking in this building" or "Smoking is permitted only in a designated smoking area." A sign for use in designated smoking areas within buildings stated: "Smoking permitted in this area only."

Several local printing firms also worked with the health department to produce signs. Their advertising gave the bylaw more exposure.

The health department, Lung Association and the Airspace organization segmented the market that had to be reached before the bylaw came into effect for work-places, and then set out to reach people in a variety of ways.

Several conferences on the development of work-place policies, held by the Lung Association, included information on the economic, legal and health aspects of a policy. The economic costs of allowing smoking in the work-place and the legal implications of allowing nonsmoking employees to be exposed to environmental tobacco smoke were important

Figure 10. Sign distributed by the Vancouver City Health Department to all businesses in the city for use at the entrances of their premises. Size shown here is one-third of actual size. Courtesy of Vancouver City Health Department.

subjects for owners of businesses. Including these topics helped business owners appreciate that a work-place policy to restrict smoking made good business sense.

Lung Association staff was involved in contacting health and human resource professionals and committees in industry and commerce which had been set up to deal with the issue of smoking in their work-place.

Health department staff made presentations to business associations, management and supervisory organizations, physical plant managers, and heating and ventilation consultants. The American Society of Heating, Refrigeration and Air-Conditioning Engineers (ASHRAE) held a one-day televised conference on the environmental considerations of ETS for its members and the public.

In October 1986, three months after the original mailing of the information on the bylaw to all businesses, the health department sent further information. This second mailing to businesses included a letter from the medical health officer emphasizing that a high level of public support had been received for the bylaw and that it made good business sense to provide a safe and comfortable environment. Enclosed with this letter was information on the health consequences of second-hand and sidestream smoke and a decal which business owners were encouraged to put on an outside door of their work-places. This decal which measured six by 12 inches (15 by 30 centimeters) said "No smoking in this building," and included the international sign for nonsmoking and the words "City of Vancouver Health Bylaw — Maximum Fine $2000." The decal was larger than credit card decals which are also put on the doors of businesses. This size meant that the "No smoking" decals were easily seen.

To ensure ongoing education about the bylaw, the city's permits and licenses staff gave information about the requirements of the bylaw to all individuals who were applying for licenses related to business premises.

By December 1986, the health department had received over 7000 telephone calls concerning the bylaw. Of these, only 30 were opposed to it. Information on the telephone inquiries was given to the media on an ongoing basis.

Step 9: Plan for Enforcement

The planned enforcement process encouraged individuals

Figure 11. Brochure printed by the City of Vancouver to inform the public about the new bylaw restricting smoking. Courtesy Vancouver City Health Department.

to become involved in promoting the bylaw and to take the responsibility to assert themselves. The first step was for a member of the public to approach the person or business owner who they felt was not complying with the bylaw. If this approach did not meet with success or if the person was uncomfortable in making this approach, a report could be made to the health department.

For alleged problems concerning public places, an inspector would make an on-site inspection on receipt of a complaint.

In the case of a complaint about a work-place, a form letter and a pamphlet containing information on the bylaw regulations were sent out to the business concerned. A copy of the letter was sent to the home address of the complainant who was given the telephone number of the environmental health inspector for the area concerned. The complainant was asked to contact the health department again if he or she felt that no corrective action had been taken by the business within two to three weeks.

If a follow-up complaint was received or if several complaints were received about the same business, the health inspector would then make either a telephone contact or a personal visit to the business to review the requirements under the bylaw, discuss a solution, and indicate how compliance would be monitored.

If the business continued to be non-compliant, a "Medical Health Officer's Order to Comply" was issued to the business. This was the beginning of a legal process and if the business continued to be non-compliant, prosecution of the business would be initiated.

Step 10. Evaluate Effect of Bylaw and Plan Follow-up

The first 12 months that the bylaw was in effect were planned to be more educational and promotional than enforcing in nature. Approximately 1000 formal complaints were received by the health department in the first year, and all of these were resolved at the early stages of the enforcement process.

Before the bylaw came into effect, a survey by the Lung Association indicated that over 60 percent of retail stores were aware of the bylaw and had taken, or were planning to take, appropriate measures to comply with it.

An informal survey by Airspace found that by late December, cigarette sales of some tobacco store owners had fallen by about 20 percent while candy sales had increased about15 percent.

The positive public acceptance of the bylaw was communicated to the prime minister and all members of parliament through a letter from the mayor of Vancouver. This letter also requested that they implement progressive federal laws to promote nonsmoking.

During the coming years, it will be necessary to take some new initiatives in order to keep the bylaw in the public eye. These may include amending some sections of the bylaw or starting legal procedures against some chronic offenders. The timing of these initiatives is important and, as in the past, other related issues happening at the provincial or national level may be useful in promoting the importance of the issue of exposure to ETS. One such example is the plan for all federal work-places in Canada to be smoke-free by January 1989. This may provide the background for further initiatives at the municipal level in the city of Vancouver.

Rating Scale for Ordinances/Bylaws

A rating scale has been devised so that individuals can rate the strength of their local ordinance/bylaw for the provision of smoke-free indoor areas for members of their community. Each type of indoor location is considered and rated according to the level of protection from environmental tobacco smoke offered to those present in each area through the wording of the local ordinance or bylaw.

Each type of indoor area is rated on a scale of zero to four points. Zero points are given when the ordinance does not include any mention of the indoor area, either in particular or in general. For example, the definition of work-place in the ordinance may or may not include a factory. Some ordinances covering work-places only include provisions for office spaces while others include factories.

The ordinance is given a rating of one point for those types of indoor areas which are mentioned in the bylaw but given very limited provisions. Here the wording of the ordinance gives support to the proprietor or person in authority who designates a smoking area, but in these cases the proprietor may designate the entire indoor area for smoking. Therefore, there may or may not be any smoke-free areas in the indoor space.

The ordinance is given a rating of two points when it specifies that smoking must not be allowed in any area other than a designated area, and that this designated area cannot be the entire indoor space. For the type of indoor area covered by these sections of the ordinance there will be some space, even though it may be minimal, where no smoking is allowed in the facility.

Three points are allotted to the indoor areas covered by the ordinance where not only is smoking allowed only in designated areas, but these areas must be separately ventilated and must be areas to which nonsmokers do not need access. In these indoor facilities, although environmental tobacco smoke does exist, on the whole nonsmokers are given some protection from it.

The ordinance is given a four-point rating for those indoor areas which it designates as totally smoke-free. That is, no smoking is allowed in the building or vehicle.

In some cases, the sections covered by the ordinance will not be easily classified using the criteria for each point level. For example, under "public transportation," buses but not trains may be covered by the ordinance. In this case, the "comments" section can be used to include this type of information. A rating may be given according to the level of protection from ETS provided to the public in most types of public transportation in the area.

A total of 25 types of indoor areas are included on the rating scale so that the possible total of rating points is 100. It must be kept in mind, however, that for each individual the exposure to the various indoor areas differs. For example, for a child in a day-care facility several days a week, the provisions for a smoke-free area in day-cares is extremely important, whereas to many adults, exposure to ETS in this type of facility would not be significant. The opposite would be true for adults in a work-place setting.

The number of people using each type of indoor area and the length of time they remain in it also varies. It must be kept in mind that no safe level of exposure to ETS has been established. To provide maximum protection from ETS for members of the community, the ordinance should include all indoor areas not under private jurisdiction .

In addition to restricting smoking in public areas and

work-places, some ordinances give provisions for signage, enforcement and public education. These can help to make the ordinance more effective. The criteria for a rating of zero or four for these three items follow. Ordinances which do not meet the criteria for a rating of either zero or four are given a ranking between these numbers according to the provisions of the ordinance related to each item.

For signage, a score of zero indicates that the ordinance makes no provisions for the use of signs and a score of four indicates that the rules for the use of signs are easily identified in the ordinance and that signs are readily available.

Enforcement provisions are rated zero if there are no provisions made for this in the ordinance. If the ordinance clearly indicates the persons or department who will enforce the ordinance and the consequences of not complying with it, the ordinance is rated four for enforcement provisions.

Public education about the ordinance may not be included in the actual wording of the ordinance but monies may have been set aside by the municipality for this purpose. A score of zero is given where no education on the ordinance is planned or has been provided by the municipality. A score of four is given where education of the public has been well planned, or has been provided in such a way that all members of the public have easy access to information which is readily understood. This information should be made available in verbal as well as written form, and should be provided in the predominant languages of the people living in the area. In areas with a large number of tourists, measures to inform visitors about the ordinance should also be considered.

Summary of Rating Scale

The ordinance or bylaw is rated for coverage of each indoor area using the following criteria. Where the scale is to be used again in the future to follow the progress of amendments to the ordinance, add the date the rating occurs.

Points for public areas and work-places:

0 - No restrictions on smoking covered by ordinance/bylaw.

1 - Provision for designated area but proprietor/person in authority may designate unlimited space for smoking area.

2 - Proprietor/person in authority must not allow smoking except in designated area(s) and this is defined as less than the total area.

3 - Same as above but also the designated area for smoking must be separately ventilated and must be an area to which nonsmokers do not need access.

4 - No smoking allowed in the indoor area.

Provisions for signage, enforcement and public education are also rated on a scale of zero to four.

A sample of the use of this rating scale is seen in Table 5 where the City of Vancouver bylaw is rated.

Table 5

Rating of the Vancouver City Bylaw, February 1988

Area	Rating
1. Restaurants	3
2. Public area of government offices	3
3. Public area of financial institutions	3
4. Reception/waiting areas	3
5. Service lines/counters	4
6. Elevators/escalators/stairways/hallways	3[a]
7. Health care offices/ facilities e.g., hospitals, medical/dental clinics,health departments	3
8. Nursing homes/extended care facilities	3
9. Child-care facilities	3
10. Waiting rooms for public transportation	3
11. Public transportation except school buses and taxis e.g., buses, ferries	4
12. School buses	4
13. Taxis	3[b]
14. Places of public assembly for entertainment, education, worship, business e.g., libraries, theaters, museums, churches, auditoriums	3
15. Places of public assembly for recreation e.g., arenas, gymnasiums	3
16. Bowling alleys, pool/billiard halls	1
17. Public meetings	4
18. Licensed premises e.g.,bars, canteens, night clubs, taverns	1
19. Public area of retail stores/outlets (excluding those exclusively selling tobacco)	4
20. Common area of shopping centers/malls	3
21. Public washrooms	4
22. Personal service establishments e.g., beauty/ barber shops, health spas, tanning studios	3
23. Educational institutions e.g., schools, colleges, universities	3
24. Work-places/places of employment frequented by the general public e.g., offices	3

25. Work-places/places of employment not frequented by the public e.g., mills, warehouses, factories	3
Total number of points (out of 100):	77
Signage provisions	5[c]
Enforcement provisions	5
Public education provisions	4[d]

Comments:

a. No smoking is permitted in elevators and stairways.

b. Smoking is permitted in a taxi with the consent of all passengers and the driver.

c. Signs continue to be made available from Health Inspectors and from several printing companies and an air conditioning company in Vancouver.

d. Written information was distributed to the public from a variety of sources and further information was available by telephone. As well as providing a copy of the bylaw, the public brochure also gave a summary of the information which was more understandable to the general public. However, there was limited information available in any language other than English, and many Vancouverites come from different ethnic backgrounds.

Figure 12. Two examples of signs which were available to businesses in Vancouver from a local air conditioning company. The one on the top includes a red circle and slash to denote "no smoking". The one on the bottom includes a green circle and is used to designate a smoking area. Courtesy of Extech Systems Limited.

Chapter 8 : State/Provincial and Federal Laws

In addition to local legislation, some countries and jurisdictions within countries, have passed laws which control the use and sale of tobacco. Some of these measures will have an indirect effect on exposure to ETS but those of direct importance are the laws restricting smoking in public places and work-places and the control of advertising and promotion.

Laws restricting where smoking may occur and restricting advertising and promotion of tobacco products will help to change the lingering perception of smoking as a glamourous, sexy, mature thing to do. Instead the public's perception of smoking will be increasingly realistic where it is seen as an addictive behavior which harms the health of those who actively smoke and of those who, often unwillingly, breathe air contaminated with ETS.

Both of these types of legislation will also help to make the behavioral norm of nonsmoking the perceived social norm as well. Although the majority of people in North America do not smoke, it is still taken for granted in some areas that a person can smoke anywhere.

When it is taken for granted that a person can breathe air not contaminated by ETS, then nonsmoking will be the social norm.

Present Status of Laws Related to Smoking Restrictions in the United States and Canada

Neither the United States nor Canada has legislated a ban on smoking in public places or in work-places. In Canada, two bills which could affect advertising of tobacco products and restrict smoking in some work-places have passed second reading in the House of Commons and, as this book goes to print, are awaiting third, and final, reading.

The first of these Bills, Bill C-204, is the Nonsmokers' Health Act which regulates smoking in federal work-places and on common carriers and amends the Hazardous Products Act in relation to cigarette advertising. This bill, which will come into effect on a proclaimed day or days, will prohibit smoking in all work-places under federal jurisdication except in designated areas, which are areas not normally occupied by nonsmokers. Designated areas in buildings built after January 1, 1990 are to be enclosed and independently ventilated.

Under this proposed act, no smoking is allowed in an enclosed space, except in a designated room, in an aircraft on a flight over 2 hours in length, a ship, railway train, or motor vehicle being operated under federal jurisdiction. In addition, tobacco and tobacco products are added to those items included in the Hazardous Products Act and conditions of sale, advertisement and importation can be regulated except where covered by the Tobacco Products Control Act. Provisions are made for further regulations to be added.

The second bill, Bill C-51, is the Tobacco Products Control Act which prohibits the advertising and promotion of tobacco products and regulates their labelling and monitoring. This Bill, if passed, will come into effect on January 1, 1989. It prohibits most forms of advertising and promotion of tobacco products. Advertising on outdoor signs would be phased out by January 1991 and retail displays by January 1993. The use of brand names in sponsorship of sports and cultural events would be allowed only for contracts signed before January 25, 1988. Free distribution of tobacco products and the use of tobacco as rewards or in contests is prohibited. The bill limits the use of the trade mark on products other than the tobacco product for which it was designed.

Each tobacco product package is to contain a list of the names and amounts of each toxic substance in the tobacco and the resulting smoke. A leaflet on the health effects of the product may be required inside the package. The list of substances along with the volume of tobacco sold and the funds spent on advertising signs and sponsorships is to be reported to the government annually.

Both of these bills were addressed by a parliamentary committee which heard briefs presented by various individuals and organizations. These briefs presented arguments as to why the bills should be passed or why they should either be amended or not passed into law. In addition, major lobby efforts have been carried out across the country by health organizations and the tobacco companies to encourage the public to contact their elected representatives to the federal government and ask for support for their particular point of view.

It is interesting to note that in 1904 and in 1971 efforts were made to pass legislation in Canada which would have controlled tobacco products. During the debates on these previous bills, the arguments against them focused on restrictions of personal freedom and economic consequences. Similarly today, when we know so much more about the overwhelming health consequences of both active smoking and exposure to ETS, these same arguments are being used against Bill C-51 and Bill C-204.[1] .

Changes in the regulations for smoking on aircraft in Canada do not have to go through the parliamentary system. The Ministry of Transport changed the Aeronautics Regulations effective December 10, 1987. After that date, smoking was banned on flights of two hours or less. The regulations include any flight with a flight segment of two hours or less, and does not allow any exceptions. The flight crew is included in the regulation. There is also provision for coverage of transporter flights which means that flights originating in Canada in Canadian aircraft are covered by the regulation. This includes, for example, flights from Vancouver to Seattle, and Toronto to New York.

In the United States, similar regulations were passed by Congress and signed by the President in December 1987. These regulations come into effect on April 23, 1988 and ban smoking on flights of two hours or less in the United States. It is unknown at this time whether or not these regulations will apply to the cockpit. These regulations have a two year sunset clause and will no longer be in effect after that time unless Congress renews them.[2]

One House bill introduced during the ninety-ninth Session of Congress (H.R. 760 – the Health in Advertising Act) was to amend the Federal Cigarette Labeling and Advertising Act to prohibit advertising tobacco products on electronic communication media. This bill would make it against the law to advertise cigarettes, small cigars and other tobacco products on any electronic media which are under the jurisdiction of the Federal Communications Commission.[3] At the time of printing, this bill had not yet been passed into law. Two other bills introduced to Congress have not proceeded beyond the initial stage because of arguments against them based on the First Amendment (Freedom of Speech). One of these bills proposes a ban on advertising and the other proposes to eliminate the tax breaks tobacco companies receive on their advertising expenses.

There are provisions in both Canada and the United States to limit smoking in most federal buildings to designated areas. These came into effect in February 1987 in the United States and cover buildings under the jurisdiction of the general services administration.[4] In Canada, a policy to restrict smoking throughout the federal public service to specially designated areas came into effect on October 1, 1987. It is expected that this will extend to a total smoke-free work-place policy on January 1, 1989.[5]

At the state level in the United States, there are only eight states (Alabama, Illinois, Louisiana, Missouri, North Carolina, Tennessee, Virginia and Wyoming) which do not have some restrictions on smoking in public places. A report on the status of smoking and health in the U.S. notes that the states of Alaska, Florida, Minnesota, Montana, Nebraska, and Utah have the most comprehensive legislation to restrict smoking. These states prohibit or restrict smoking to designated areas of public meetings, public transportation vehicles, restaurants, retail stores, cultural and recreational facilities, government buildings, offices and work-places, passenger elevators, health care facilities, offices of health care practitioners, and educational facilities.[6]

Sixteen states restrict smoking in government-controlled offices and 12 states restrict smoking in private work-place settings. The type of restrictions in the work-places vary. They include: prohibiting smoking in all places of employment where a "no smoking" sign is posted; requiring employers, on request, to provide employees with work-spaces where smoking is not allowed; requiring employers to determine a policy on smoking and post written rules; and prohibiting smoking in work-places except in designated areas. Four states ban smoking in jury deliberation rooms.[7]

Quebec is the only province or territory in Canada which has a law restricting smoking in public places. Manitoba has legislation being considered for passage in 1988. There are no provinces or territories in Canada with legislation which restricts smoking in the work-place. This type of restriction only exists at the local level in some municipalities.

Rating a State/Provincial Law

The rating scale previously introduced in this book for use with ordinances or municipal bylaws can also be used to measure the strength of the provisions of a state or provincial law which restricts smoking in public places and work-places. As these laws apply to indoor areas in a much larger jurisdiction than a local ordinance, they have, on the whole, been less restrictive. Also, state/provincial laws may override local ordinances and, therefore, they tend to be less specific in their wording. Some important items to notice in state and provincial laws are provisions for indoor areas that cannot be covered in local legislation. This may include transportation systems between cities and some government offices.

Table 6 is a rating of one state law. The Washington State Clean Indoor Air Act came into effect on July 28, 1985. More information on the use of the rating scale can be found in Chapter 7 in the section "Rating Scale for Ordinances/Bylaws."

What You Can Do to Promote a State/Provincial Law

Where state/provincial laws exist, you can use the previously noted rating guide to determine the level of protection from ETS that the current law affords you. For those who are not covered by a state/provincial law, and where there is public support for such an law (for example, as seen by the existence of various local ordinances or bylaws in the state/

Table 6

Rating of the Washington State Clean Indoor Air Act, February 1988

The following point system is used to rate the law:

Points for public areas and work-places:
0 - No restrictions on smoking covered by the law.
1 - Provision for designated area but proprietor/person in authority may designate unlimited space for smoking area.
2 - Proprietor/person in authority must not allow smoking except in designated area(s) and this is defined as less than the total area.
3 - Same as above but also the designated area for smoking must be separately ventilated and must be an area to which nonsmokers do not need access.
4 - No smoking allowed in the indoor area.
Provisions for signage, enforcement and public education area also rated on a scale of zero to four.

Area	Rating
1. Restaurants	1
2. Public area of government offices	4
3. Public area of financial institutions	4
4. Reception/waiting areas	2
5. Service lines/counters	2
6. Elevators/escalators/stairways/hallways	2[a]
7. Health care offices/facilities e.g., hospitals, medical/dental clinics, health departments	2[b]
8. Nursing homes/extended care facilities	2
9. Child-care facilities	0
10. Waiting rooms for public transportation	2
11. Public transportation except school buses and taxis e.g., buses, ferries	4[c]
12. School buses	4
13. Taxis	1
14. Places of public assembly for entertainment, education, worship, business e.g., libraries, theaters, museums, churches, auditoriums	3[d]

15. Places of public assembly for recreation e.g. arenas, gymnasiums	3
16. Bowling alleys, pool/billiard halls	1
17. Public meetings	4
18. Licensed premises e.g., bars, canteens, night clubs, taverns	1
19. Public area of retail stores/outlets (excluding those exclusively selling tobacco)	4
20. Common area of shopping centers/malls	2
21. Public washrooms	2
22. Personal service establishments e.g. beauty/barber shops, health spas, tanning studios	2
23. Educational institutions e.g., schools, colleges, universities	2[e]
24. Work-places/places of employment frequented by the general public e.g., offices	0
25. Work-places/places of employment not frequented by the public e.g., mills, warehouses, factories	0
Total number of points (out of 100)	54
Signage provisions	4[f]
Enforcement provisions	5
Public education provisions	3[g]

Comments:

a,b. No smoking allowed in any elevators or in the hallways of health care facilities.

c. Buses and street cars covered only. Ferries not included in the law.

d. No smoking allowed in museums.

e. No smoking allowed in classrooms and lecture halls.

f. Signs are readily available. However, the law does not specify size and states only that they must be "posted conspicuously."

g. No provisions were made in the act for public education but the Division of Health of the Washington State Department of Social and Health Services, together with the American Lung Association of Washington, published a brochure which explained the law and this was made available to the general public.

Figure 13. Public information brochure published jointly in 1985 by the Washington State Department of Social and Health Services and the American Lung Association of Washington.

province and by the presence of a variety of action groups promoting nonsmoking), the rating scale can give some idea of the protective measures you would like taken in your state/ province. If you decide that the present law adequately protects you from ETS, you can contact your elected representative to your state/provincial government and indicate your support and appreciation for the law. If you feel that the present law, or lack of one, is not offering you and your family sufficient protection from exposure to ETS, then contact your elected representative and indicate this. When you contact your local elected representatives and those dealing directly with health concerns, emphasize the need for strong laws protecting the public from ETS. You may want to include some of the concerns about ETS and active smoking from Chapters 1 and 2 and Appendix A, which outline what is presently known about the health consequences of active smoking and exposure to ETS.

Local health organizations and nonsmoking action groups will be interested in your concerns and appreciate your support of their efforts to promote laws which protect the public from ETS. Working with these groups is especially useful when there is little evident support in your area for such laws. You can help these groups increase the knowledge of members of your community about ETS and what is happening in other parts of the country to protect the public from exposure to it.

What You Can Do to Promote Federal Laws

In order for more progress to be made at the federal level to protect the public from exposure to ETS, elected representatives need to hear from individuals who support laws which regulate smoking in public places and work-places, and who support restrictions on the advertising and promotion of tobacco. As seen with the bills being dealt with currently in Canada, this requires an ongoing lobbying effort by members of the public and organizations. The first reading of Bill C-204 was on October 6, 1986, and for Bill C-51, April 30, 1987. Since then, strong lobbying efforts have been made against the bills. For the bills to become law, equally strong, if not stronger, efforts have been needed to influence politicians to pass them. Consistent, ongoing efforts are required from health-conscious consumers and organizations, using politically sound arguments, to promote laws which will protect the public from the promotion of the use of tobacco as a socially-esteemed behavior, and from exposure to environmental tobacco smoke.

You can act on both an individual and group level to support these types of laws. You can write or phone your elected representatives on an ongoing basis (for example, once every few months) to indicate your support for new laws. Find out what your representatives' viewpoints are on proposed legislation and either support their decisions or give them more information to try to sway their opinions to the support of health-oriented legislation. In addition, when new information becomes available on the tobacco issue, you can contact your representative to make sure that he or she is aware of this new information. At a group level, you can join and support organizations which are lobbying for new laws. To be more effective as a lobbyist, you need to keep informed. The organizations listed in Appendix C can help you in this regard, especially if you are on their mailing list for newsletters or other forms of updated information.

Sources:
1. Collishaw, N.E. **Legislative Control of Tobacco in Canada**. Notes for a presentation to the Sixth World Conference on Smoking and Health, Tokyo, Japan, November 9-12, 1987.
2. Davis, R. Office of Smoking and Health, Washington, D.C., personal communication, March 9, 1988.
3. United States Public Health Service. **Smoking and Health. A National Status Report. A Report to Congress.** U.S. Department of Health and Human Services: Washington, D.C., 1987, pp.63,64.
4. Davis, R., personal communication, March 9, 1988.
5. Treasury Board of Canada. News release on **Public Service Tobacco Policy**, April 22, 1987.
6. United States Public Health Service, p.64.
7. United States Public Health Service, p.67.

Give kids a chance

Please write your
Member of Parliament
in support of...

The National Campaign to Pass the Tobacco Products Control Act

Figure 14. Public information brochure published by the Nonsmokers' Rights Association to promote public support of Bill C-51. Distributed by groups across Canada in 1987.

Figure 15. Photograph taken of a billboard in Dublin, Ireland in September 1985. One of a series of billboard designs developed by the Irish Health Education Bureau for their "Do Knot" nonsmoking promotion campaign.

CLEARING THE AIR WORLD-WIDE

"By presenting itself to the world as a creator of wealth, a source of revenue, the supplier of jobs, the bringer of development, the provider of pleasure, the patron of sport and the arts, and the defender of freedom, the tobacco industry has successfully diverted political and public attention from the real issue at stake: that the product from which all these undoubted benefits flow has wiped out more people than all the wars of this century."
Taylor, Peter. **Smoke Ring — The Politics of Tobacco.** Bodley Head Ltd.: London, 1984. p.281.

Figure 16. Illustrations found on both sides of a tent card produced by the Calgary Health Services. The card was used by restaurants in the Calgary area during the Olympic Games in February 1988. Courtesy of Calgary Health Department.

Chapter 9 : International Nonsmoking Promotion

Approximately 70 countries have enacted legislation to provide some control over tobacco. This includes legislation which may control advertising and promotion of tobacco products, mandate the use of health warnings and product labels which include the levels of tar and nicotine in the tobacco products, and control the level of tar and nicotine in the tobacco sold in the country. Some legislation allows sales to adults only and restricts the point of sale (for example, bans sales from vending machines), increases taxes and prices, provides economic assistance to decrease reliance on tobacco as a cash crop (especially in developing countries), restricts smoking in public places and work-places, and/or mandates health education for the public about the effects of active smoking and exposure to environmental tobacco smoke.[1]

Countries which do not allow the advertising of tobacco products include Algeria, Bulgaria, Czechoslovakia, Finland, French Polynesia, the German Democratic Republic, Hungary, Iceland, Italy, Jordan, Mozambique, Norway, Poland, Romania, Singapore, Sudan, U.S.S.R., and Yugoslavia. Iceland, Spain, and Sudan have banned smoking in public places. No country has yet banned smoking in all work-places.[2]

The Third-World Market

Tobacco has not been a major crop in Third-World countries until recently. In some of these countries, it is now seen as a valuable cash crop and where, as in North America, it can bring in more money per acre or hectare than many other crops. The fact that multinational tobacco companies are willing to offer assistance with production and marketing increases its attractiveness. Individual farmers can obtain loans more easily for tobacco farming than for other crops, as potential lenders are aware that the tobacco companies' support will help to ensure the farmer's success.

Unfortunately, this can tie up a country's financial, labor and land resources in a product which has been shown to cause illness and death. Although the tobacco can mean a short-term increase in cash for the farmers and the countries, there are long-term problems associated with it.

When agricultural land is used for tobacco farming it cannot be used for food production. In some Third-World countries, increased tobacco production has led to an increased need to import food. Tobacco farming is also more labor intensive, especially when it is being harvested.

In addition, chemicals are sprayed on the tobacco fields to improve the quality of the crop. In many Third-World countries there are few, if any, regulations concerning the health and safety standards associated with this type of spraying in North America.

When tobacco is cured, wood is needed for the process. Clearing and burning of wood for this purpose in Third-World countries leads to less available firewood for fuel for other purposes like cooking and also causes erosion of the land. And, as in North America, the use of cigarettes can lead to fires, in an already depleted forested area.

The use of cigarettes often increases when they are produced in a country. Tobacco companies are advertising their products in developing countries, often using an American image, to encourage people to smoke. Tar and nicotine levels are usually higher in the cigarettes sold in Third-World countries compared to those sold in North America. The health problems resulting from smoking are compounded by the already- existing health problems of developing nations. Some of these countries already have a high infant death rate – an increase in the rate of maternal smoking has the potential for multiplying the risks associate with unhealthy pregnancies.

Concerns about the emerging Third-World market, as well as the well-known health-related concerns in developed nations, have led to world-wide action on the tobacco issue. The following are recent statements issued to give direction at the international level. The first is the statement made by the World Health Organization in 1986 and the second is the list of recommendations from the Sixth World Conference on Smoking and Health held in Tokyo, Japan, in November 1987.

World Health Organization Statement on Tobacco or Health[3]

Deeply concerned by the current pandemic of smoking and other forms of tobacco use, which results in the loss of the lives of at least one million human beings every year and in illness and suffering for many more;

Believing that the battle between health and tobacco must and can be won for the sake of human health;

Encouraged by the existence of total bans, restrictions or limitations on tobacco advertising in several countries;

1. AFFIRMS:

1) that tobacco smoking and the use of tobacco in all its forms is incompatible with the attainment of health for all by the year 2000;

2) that the presence of carcinogens and other toxic substances in tobacco smoke and other tobacco products is a known fact; and that the causal link between tobacco and a range of fatal and disabling diseases has been scientifically proven;

3) that passive, enforced or involuntary smoking violates the right to health of nonsmokers, who must be protected against this noxious form of environmental pollution;

2. CALLS for a global public health approach and action **now** to combat the tobacco pandemic;

3. DEPLORES all direct and indirect practices the aim of which is to promote the use of tobacco, as this product is addictive and dangerous even when used as promoted;

4. URGES those member states which have not yet done so to implement smoking control strategies; these, as a minimum, should contain the following:

1) measures to ensure that nonsmokers receive effecting protection, to which they are entitled, from involuntary exposure to tobacco smoke, in enclosed public places, restaurants, transport, and places of work and entertainment;

2) measures to promote abstention from the use of tobacco so as to protect children and young people from becoming addicted;

3) measures to ensure that a good example is set in all health-related premises and by all health personnel;

4) measures leading to the progressive elimination of those socioeconomic, behavioral, and other incentives which maintain and promote the use of tobacco;

5) prominent health warnings, which might include the statement that tobacco is addictive, on cigarette packets, and containers of all types of tobacco products;

6) the establishment of programs of education and public information on tobacco and health issues, including smoking cessation programs, with active involvement of the health professions and the media;

7) monitoring of trends in smoking and other forms of tobacco use, tobacco-related diseases, and effectiveness of national smoking control action;

8) the promotion of viable economic alternatives to tobacco production, trade and taxation;

9) the establishment of a national focal point to stimulate, support, and coordinate all the above activities;

5.APPEALS to other organizations of the United Nations system:

1) to support WHO in all ways possible within their fields of competence;

2) to show solidarity with WHO's efforts to stem the spread of tobacco-induced diseases by protecting the health of nonsmokers on their premises, as this action would have a major exemplar role;

3) to help member states in identifying and implementing economic alternatives to tobacco cultivation, production and trade;

6. REQUESTS the director-general:

1) to strengthen the present program on smoking and health without waiting for its official introduction in the Eighth General Program of Work, as a visible and resolute attitude on the part of WHO to provide member states with encouragement

and support, which are necessary prerequisites to abating the smoking pandemic before the year 2000;

2) to mobilize support for the present program on smoking and health in terms of funds and manpower which would ensure adequate program continuity on a long-term basis;

3) to coordinate activities in support of WHO's action on smoking and health with other organizations of the United Nations system at the highest executive level;

4) to continue and strengthen collaboration with non-governmental organizations as appropriate;

5) to ensure that WHO plays an effective global advocacy role in tobacco and health issues and that, in common with other health institutions, it plays an exemplar role in non-smoking practices;

6) to provide support to national smoking control efforts;

7) to report on progress to the executive board at its eighty-first session and to the forty-first World Health Assembly.

Recommendations of the Sixth World Conference on Smoking and Health[4]

1. IMPLEMENTATION OF PREVIOUS RECOMMENDATIONS

The conference urges implementation of all previous recommendations of WHO expert committee reports and previous world conferences.

2. TOBACCO CONTROL IN DEVELOPING COUNTRIES

a) Each country should set up a national coordinating body on tobacco control. Further recommendations are for regional and global coordination of such bodies.

b) Governments in developing countries should stop the transnational tobacco industry targetting these countries.

c) As a minimum, no promotion should be allowed that is illegal in the country of origin. Tobacco should cease to be used as a political leverage in trade matters.

d) Non-government organizations in developed countries should work to assure their own governments do not contribute to the promotion of tobacco use in developing countries.

e) Prevention should be the primary objective of national and international tobacco-control programs.

3. ENFORCED SMOKING AND NONSMOKERS' RIGHTS
All countries should work toward establishing smoke-free environments in all enclosed public places, particularly work-sites, transport, health-care facilities, schools, and child-care facilities.

4. LEGISLATION AND PRODUCT LIABILITY SUITS
a) Tobacco-control legislation should be seen as an integral part of a comprehensive tobacco-control policy.
b) Scientific and medical organizations should be urged to help, support and encourage groups that are freer to lobby and take a more activist role.
c) The conference endorses the legitimacy of victims (and their families) of tobacco-induced diseases to obtain compensation from tobacco manufacturers through judicial processes. Governments should seek reimbursement for all medical and other relevant costs which they have to bear by taking care of the victims of tobacco use.

5. SMOKELESS TOBACCO
Smokeless tobacco should be banned in all countries where it is not yet an established habit. In countries where neither the traditional nor new forms of smokeless tobacco are established, all possible restrictions on advertising, promotion, and sale, linked with health education and tax policy, should be introduced immediately.

6.TOBACCO AND ECONOMICS
a) Pro-health organizations should review the socio-economic and health costs of tobacco use to the individual and to the society.
b) All countries should regularly increase taxation on tobacco products as a health policy measure.
c) All appropriate bodies should consider higher insurance rates for smokers to reflect the true socio-economic and health costs of smoking.

7. TOBACCO AND WOMEN
The issue of women and smoking should be integrated into local, national and international tobacco-control strategies and health education programs, with women serving on all anti-tobacco committees.

8. TOBACCO AND CHILDREN

a) There should be increased international cooperation on research into tobacco use by children, especially regarding influences on smoking behavior, with a specific recommendation for international workshops on this topic.

b) The conference proposes that, on a country and global basis, the number of children alive today who will be unnecessarily killed by tobacco be estimated and these figures made public.

9. TOBACCO CESSATION

Every country should recognize the complex nature of tobacco use and should implement appropriate and demonstrably effective cessation techniques.

10. WORLD HEALTH ORGANIZATION

Delegates from each country should request that their health ministers support a larger and more dynamic role for the World Health Organization Program on Tobacco or Health.

11. PROMOTION

a) All forms of tobacco advertising, sponsorship and any other direct and indirect forms of promotion in all media be banned in all countries. This conference urges governments to ban television tobacco advertising as a first step toward a total ban.

b) The conference recommends that all sporting events be smoke-free and free from all tobacco advertising and promotion. In particular it is noted that promotion of tobacco products in Olympic Games violates the Olympic Charter and whereas enforced smoking is known to be detrimental to athletic performance and inconsistent with the healthful image of the Olympic Games, the Sixth World Conference on Smoking and Health recommends to the International Olympic Committee that all future summer and winter Olympic Games adopt the smoke-free model of the 1988 Calgary Winter Games.

Sources:

1. Roemer, R. "Legislative action to control smoking – Accomplishments and challenges" in Skirrow, J.(editor). **Strategies for a Smoke-Free World. Selected Resource Documents from the International Workshop on Smoking and Health.**

Calgary, Alberta 1985. Alberta Alcohol and Drug Abuse Commission: Edmonton, Alberta, 1986. pp.63-84.
2. Roemer, R., p.97-101.
3. Statement issued from the fourteenth plenary session, May 15,1986, Agenda item 22, executive board meeting, World Health Assembly, World Health Organization, Geneva, Switzerland, quoted from **Chronic Disease in Canada**. 7(2):35,36, September 1986.
4. Recommendations distributed on a handout to the delegates at the conclusion of the conference in Tokyo in November 1987.

References on Third-World Market:
Madeley, J. "The environmental impact of tobacco production in developing countries." **New York State Journal of Medicine.** 83(12):1310-1313.
Muller, M. "Preventing tomorrow's epidemic — The control of smoking and tobacco production in developing countries." **New York State Journal of Medicine.** 83(12):1304-1309.
Smoking Control Strategies in Developing Countries: Report of a WHO Expert Committee. Technical Report Series 695. World Health Organization: Geneva, 1983.
Taylor, P. **Smoke Ring — The Politics of Tobacco**. Bodley Head:London, 1984.

Chapter 10 : A New Nonsmoking Promotion Initiative

Various individuals, groups, organizations and governments are working together to increase the number of situations where people can enjoy an environment which is free of environmental tobacco smoke. Often a new idea comes from an individual and then many people work together to develop a program from the idea. The program is tried out in one area, its level of success measured, and then information about the program is shared with others. An example of a program where this approach was taken is the Winter Olympic Games Fresh Air Program. Although this program took place in one area of Alberta, Canada, it has the potential for influencing sports and other events internationally.

XV Winter Olympic Games Fresh Air Program

The Winter Olympic Games in Calgary in February 1988 were the first modern Olympics with smoke-free spaces. The initiative for the Fresh Air Program came from Dr. John Read, Professor of Community Health Sciences and Pediatrics at the University of Calgary. With the assistance and cooperation of other individuals, organizations and governments, Read proceeded to make the program a reality. The following information about the Olympic Games Fresh Air program was obtained through an interview with him.

Read is a medical doctor whose family has been involved with the Canadian Ski Association for many years. His wife is a former Canadian champion skier and two of his sons are World Cup and Olympic skiers. Read's combined interests in health and in skiing led him to be very concerned when, to his dismay, in 1983, the Canadian Ski Association accepted sponsorship from a tobacco company for a five-year period. Distressed about this link of amateur sport with a product which causes so much illness and death, Read campaigned with others in the Ski Association to change the sponsorship. At the association's annual meeting in 1984, this concerned group put forward a motion that the sponsorship from the tobacco company be discontinued. In a meeting attended by approximately 400 people, their motion was defeated by two votes. As a result, the Canadian Ski Association continued to be sponsored by a tobacco company until 1988.

Although the move to block the sponsorship failed, the effort was successful in bringing together concerned people from various groups who spoke out publicly against the sponsorship. It resulted in the formation of Physicians for a Smoke-free Canada, which began with the 27 physicians who were involved with the ski team. The sponsorship issue also prompted people from the national health organizations to start speaking out as advocates for nonsmoking, and health-related groups began working cooperatively on the tobacco issue.

The concern of these groups and the media attention paid to the sponsorship issue later prompted the Minister of Health in Canada to announce that any amateur sport organization which accepted new sponsorship from a tobacco company would not receive any funding from the government body, Fitness and Amateur Sport. Over the five years of their contract with the tobacco company – 1983 to 1988 – the Canadian Ski Association received over $500,000 from Fitness and Amateur Sport.[1]

Nonsmoking and the Winter Olympics in Calgary

With this background of concern about the combining of tobacco and amateur sport, when the Winter Olympic Games were awarded to Calgary, his home town, Read set about to try to ensure that the Olympics would be linked with nonsmoking rather than smoking. After the problems with the Canadian Ski Association and tobacco sponsorship, no sponsorship or advertisements from tobacco companies were accepted by the Olympic Committee. However, Read wanted to go one step further and initiated the idea of the Fresh Air Program for the Olympic Games which would ensure that those participating in the Games were provided with a smoke-free environment.

The Fresh Air Program had three objectives. The first objective was to protect the athletes from exposure to environmental tobacco smoke. After training for years to reach a peak in their performance for the Olympic Games, the ability of the athletes could be decreased by exposure to ETS, which contains carbon monoxide as well as many other poisonous and irritating substances. This exposure could occur in the athletes' village, on the way to the competition, or in the starting area for the event unless steps were taken to ensure the air in these places was smoke-free.

The second objective was to provide smoke-free spaces for participants, officials, coaches and spectators. Many people in the population have medical conditions, such as heart disease, asthma, bronchitis, and other respiratory diseases, which are made worse by exposure to ETS. This effect can occur even if a person is exposed to ETS for a short period of time.

Most people at the Olympic Games would be nonsmokers and should be able to participate in a healthful, smoke-free environment. At least 33 of the 57 participating countries had legislation to control smoking. It was therefore felt that most people attending the Games would be very familiar with the concept of smoke-free spaces.

The third objective of the program was to preserve the dignity and healthful image of the Olympic Games. The Olympic Charter promotes the idea of setting an example for the youth of the world. With the emphasis on a drug-free Olympics, it would be inappropriate to ignore one of the most addictive drugs available – nicotine.

Permitting smoking to occur in the areas where competition took place would mean that smoking would probably be seen frequently in the media, and would therefore be associated with the Games. On the other hand, by emphasizing the use of smoke-free spaces, nonsmoking and smoke-free policies would be associated with the Games. To reach this objective, outdoor as well as indoor areas had to be covered by the program.

Approval of the Olympic Committee and Funding for Evaluation

Read first approached the Olympic Calgary Olympique (OCO) board of directors with the idea of the Fresh Air Program in 1986. This board consisted of 27 Canadians – former athletes, businessmen and politicians – who were responsible for the organization of the Games in Calgary. Read was already known by the Chairman of OCO, Frank King, for his work on the alpine site selection committee for the Olympics. Read found that King was very supportive of the idea of the Fresh Air Program.

As the idea of the Fresh Air Program spread, letters were received from across Canada, the United States, Great Britain, and other countries supporting it. As a result, many of the pre-Olympic events adopted the idea of smoke-free spaces. The circumstances at other pre-Olympic events increased support for the Fresh Air Program. For example, the 1987 World Speed Skating Championships in the Netherlands were held in an indoor skating oval like the one in Calgary. This oval was filled with tobacco smoke during the competition. This emphasized the need for smoke-free spaces for the athletes and brought more support for the Olympic Games Fresh Air Program.

Read was a member of the medical committee that reported to OCO and this medical group presented the Olympic Games Fresh Air Program to OCO for approval in 1987. The support was almost unanimous and the program was launched.

The next week, Read's son, Ken, (a former member of Canada's ski team known as the Crazy Canucks) took this information to Budapest, Hungary, for a meeting of the Athletes Advisory Commission. This is an independent group of Olympic athletes who work with the Olympic organization on an international scale. This group of athletes passed a motion to endorse OCO's decision.

As the Olympic Games Fresh Air Program was a new idea with a great deal of potential to promote the link between nonsmoking and sports, Read wanted the program's effectiveness to be evaluated. This would mean that the outcomes of the program in Calgary would be identified and the information could then be used by others who wanted to promote similar programs. Read was on the executive board of the Canadian Council on Smoking and Health (CCSH) and he approached this organization for support for the program and its evaluation. The CCSH and Read approached the Canadian government for funding to evaluate the success of the program. This funding was approved late in 1987 and four people were hired to carry out the evaluation process.

The Fresh Air Program

All competition areas and most sites and facilities were smoke-free with smoking limited to specially designated areas. Smoking was not permitted by officials, volunteers, or athletes within the confines of the actual events — indoor or outdoor. In addition, smoking by spectators was prohibited within the confines of all indoor events.

Smoke-free spaces included:

• OLYMPIC VILLAGES: These villages for the athletes at the University of Calgary and the Canmore Nordic Centre were smoke-free except for a designated area in each center.

• TRANSPORTATION: All vehicles operated by the OCO '88 transportation department were posted as nonsmoking areas as well as the load and unload zones at all ski events, access elevators to and within sport facilities, and the City of Calgary transportation vehicles.

• MEDICAL FACILITIES: All medical facilities under the direction of the medical service program were nonsmoking areas. The Foothills Hospital, the site of the drug control laboratory and the main referral center for emergency treatment, already had a smoke-free policy.

•VENUES: Smoking by officials (including volunteers), coaches or athletes was not allowed within the vicinity of the competition areas (start buildings, gatekeeping and access control areas, race offices and secretariat). Designated smoking areas were identified within each competition area.

•LODGES: All day lodges were considered part of the venue.

•RESTAURANT AREAS: All eating areas serving athletes and officials were posted as nonsmoking areas.

•OLYMPIC VOLUNTEER CENTER: This center was designated as a nonsmoking facility, except for certain posted areas. Nonsmoking rules and regulations were in effect during competition and planning meetings (meetings of a jury, officials, or team captains).

•MEDIA WORK CENTERS: Separate smoking areas were designated by the use of appropriate signs within each setting.

Sponsorship by manufacturers of tobacco products was not allowed and advertising of tobacco products was not permitted at the competition areas or on "equipment used in the Olympic Games, nor on the uniforms or numbers worn by contestants or officials" (Olympic Charter Rule 6, Bylaw 8 and Rule 53, Bylaw 10).

Letting People Know

Information about the XV Olympic Games Fresh Air Program was included in the information packages sent to all of the participants in the Games, including the 1750 athletes, prior to the event. The information was made available in the official languages of the participating countries. The press and media in some countries (for example, Great Britain, Switzerland, and the Scandinavian countries) ran articles about the program prior to the Games. Press releases about the program were developed for, and distributed to, all Winter Olympic countries. The sports federations and national Olympic committees in each country also spread the word about the program.

In Canada, press coverage was given to the program several weeks before the Games. At that time, the Minister of National Health and Welfare, Jake Epp, announced the Olympic Games Fresh Air Program and the sports-related Smoke-Free All-stars Program at a media event in Calgary.

All of the OCO staff and volunteers in the Calgary area were made aware of the program in their meetings.

To remind people about the program, international signage was used in all areas associated with the Games. These varied from large, fixed signs to signs on stands which could be used in tents and outdoor areas. Read worked with the architects and interior decorators for the Games to make sure the size, color and mounting of the signs were appropriate for their purpose (letting people know which areas were smoke-free and which ones were designated smoking areas), as well as fitting into the decor of each venue. Two thousand decals were used in transportation vehicles. As well as the international symbols (a red circle and slash across a cigarette to indicate nonsmoking, and a green circle around a cigarette to indicate smoking), the signs had a variety of written messages such as "Smoking restricted to designated areas only", "This facility is under the OCO '88 Fresh Air Policy. Your cooperation is appreciated", and "Smoking permitted — designated area." The total cost for the program, including signage, for the Games was approximately $25,000. It is expected that some, if not all of this cost, was offset by savings in ashtray purchases and cleaning and fire insurance costs.

Evaluation of the Program

Through information packages, the media, and signs, all of those at the Winter Games in Calgary were made aware of the expectation that they would not smoke except in designated areas. The program then relied on all of those at the Games to enforce the policy themselves. The evaluation planned for the program was to measure the effectiveness of this strategy.

Four types of studies were carried out. First of all, air quality studies of indoor sites were done at various times using a Piezo Electric Balance Portable Analyzer. This machine measures, by weight, the tiny particles in the air which are 0.01 to three microns in diameter. ETS is not the only source of these particles, but the weight measurement increases as the level of ETS rises.[2]

Secondly, individuals' awareness of the program and their level of acceptance of it were studied through the use of interviews and observation. Next, attitudes by type of participant, sport, and country of origin were studied, using interviews and observation. Finally, awareness of the program and compliance was studied at outdoor events using observation, interviews, and questionnaires.

It is anticipated that Read will present the results of the evaluation of the Olympic Games Fresh Air Program to the World Health Organization in September 1988, and then to the people who are involved in planning the next Winter Olympic Games in Albertville, France.

Future Plans

Interest has been expressed by those in Albertville, France to consider a Fresh Air program for the next Winter Olympics. Those involved with the Summer Olympics in Seoul, Korea in 1988 have also contacted Read about the program. In Barcelona, Spain, the committee organizing the next Summer Olympics (in 1992) has already accepted a tobacco company as a sponsor. However, health organizations in the area are lobbying this group to promote the Olympic Charter and its stated exemption of tobacco companies as sponsors.

It has been proposed that, once the results of the Olympic Games Fresh Air Program are reviewed, a manual be written on how to promote and carry out a Fresh Air program for both sports and cultural events. This manual would be made available to individuals and organizations wanting to carry out a similar program in their own area.

Sources:

1. According to the staff at Fitness and Amateur Sport, the funding made available to the Canadian Ski Association for the fiscal years between March 1983, and to date in February 1988, totalled $552,672, personal communication, February 1988.

2. This information on the Piezo Electric Balance Portable Analyzer was obtained from Neil Collishaw, Chief, Tobacco Products Unit, Environmental Health Directorate, Health Protection Branch, Health and Welfare Canada during a telephone conversation on February 5, 1988.

Appendix A : True-False Statements and Answers based on the Surgeons General's Reports

The following true-false statements and answers indicate some of the findings that have been covered in the reports of the Surgeons General from 1980 to 1986. The material is arranged by date and the content matter of each report. Decide whether each statement in a section is true or false and then refer to the "answers" section to find out how aware you are of the health consequences of active smoking and the use of smokeless tobacco. Information from the Surgeon General's report of 1986, which reviewed studies on the risks related to involuntary smoking, is found in Chapter 2.

1980 - Health Consequences of Smoking for Women

True-False Statements

__ 1. Widespread use of cigarettes among men in North America started about 20 to 30 years before their use became widespread among women.

__ 2. The proportion of men who smoke has decreased more rapidly since 1965 than that for women, with the result that the percentage of men and women who smoke is now almost equal.

__ 3. A pregnant woman's smoking can have a significant effect on the weight of her baby.

__ 4. A pregnant woman's smoking does not affect the amount of oxygen reaching her unborn baby.

__ 5. A mother's cigarette smoking can lead to premature delivery of her baby.

__ 6. Parental smoking does not affect the baby after it is born.

__ 7. Women who smoke are more likely to suffer from ulcers, chronic sinus infections, chronic bronchitis, emphysema, heart disease and be absent from work more than women who do not smoke.

__ 8. Women who use birth control pills and smoke are 10 times more likely to have heart disease than women who do not smoke and do not take birth control pills.

__ 9. Cancer of the mouth, throat, larynx, esophagus, kidney and bladder, as well as cancer of the lung, are linked to cigarette smoking in women.

__10. Excessive use of alcohol can increase the risk of certain types of cancer in people who smoke.

__11. Women who smoke weigh, on average, 10 to 20 pounds (4.5 to 9 kilograms) less than women who do not smoke.

__12. The lung cancer rate for women is no longer increasing.

Answers

1. True. Around the turn of the century men replaced other forms of tobacco with cigarettes. By the end of the First World War, about 50 percent of adult males were cigarette smokers. This resulted in an increase in the number of lung cancer deaths seen during and after the 1930s. Since the widespread use of cigarettes by women did not start until the onset of the Second World War, the increase in the number of lung cancer deaths was seen much later in women. Since women and men now have similar smoking habits, the level of smoking-related disease in both men and women can be expected to be comparable in years to come unless there is a change in this "equality" of smoking habits.

2. True. From 1965 to 1978, the proportion of adult male cigarette smokers fell from 51 to 37 percent while the proportion of adult female cigarette smokers remained almost the same with a change from 33 to 30 percent.

3. True. The risk of having a low birthweight baby (under 5.5 pounds or 2500 grams) is 53 percent higher for a light smoker and 130 percent higher for a heavy smoker than it is for a nonsmoker. If a woman quits smoking early in her pregnancy, her risk of having a low birthweight baby is similar to that of a nonsmoker. On average, women who smoke have babies who weigh 7 ounces, or 200 grams, less than those of women who do not smoke. This growth-retarding effect on the unborn baby may affect the child's long-term growth and development.

4. False. Although the baby is smaller, the placenta is thinner, larger and heavier in mothers who smoke and it also undergoes a more rapid aging process. This is probably in response to the decrease in the oxygen reaching the baby. Women who smoke are more likely to lose their baby during the pregnancy, at birth or soon after the baby is born. This may be due to lack of oxygen or breathing problems in an otherwise normal infant.

5. True. Smoking increases a woman's chances of having problems like bleeding early or late in her pregnancy, problems with where the placenta is attached to the uterus (or womb), early or prolonged rupture of the membranes around the baby, and premature delivery. All of these carry a risk to the baby. Up to 14 percent of all premature deliveries may be due to maternal smoking. Premature deliveries account for a large proportion of deaths in very young infants.

6. False. Infants of mothers who smoke are hospitalized more for pneumonia and bronchitis during their first year of life than infants of mothers who do not smoke. Children of parents who smoke tend to be hospitalized more frequently, have more visits to the doctor, and have longer stays in hospital than do children of parents who do not smoke. Also, children whose parents smoke are more likely to smoke themselves.

7. True. Women who smoke have more chronic bronchitis and/or emphysema, chronic sinus infection, ulcers, arteriosclerotic heart disease, chronic obstructive lung disease, chronic cough and phlegm production, and poorer lung function than women who do not smoke. They also have a 20 percent higher incidence of acute conditions like flu and lose more days from work due to illness and injury. Women who

have at some time smoked are more likely to have to limit their activity before the age of 65 compared to women who have never smoked.

8. True. Coronary heart disease (which includes heart attacks) occurs, in general, about twice as often in women who smoke than in those who do not. Women who use birth control pills and smoke increase their risk to 10 times that of women who do not smoke. Women who smoke low tar and nicotine cigarettes lessen their risk for coronary heart disease, but their risk is still considerably more than that of women who do not smoke.

9. True. Cigarette smoking is linked with cancer of the lung, mouth and throat, voice box (larynx), and esophagus in both men and women and with cancer of the kidney and bladder in women. By 1980, cigarette smoking accounted for 25 percent of all cancer deaths in women. Once a woman has quit smoking for 10 to 15 years, her risk of developing cancer of the lung and larynx is similar to that of a nonsmoker.

10. True. Excessive use of alcohol along with cigarette smoking increases the risk of cancer of the voice box, mouth and throat to more than that found with cigarette smoking alone.

11. False. Women who smoke weigh, on average, only 1.2 to 4.5 pounds (0.5 to 2 kg.) less than women who do not smoke. Smoking is, therefore, not a major factor in weight control. The use of exercise and good nutrition are not only more effective means to reduce weight, if this is required, but they also tend to increase the person's feeling of well-being, rather than increasing the risk of illness.
In one study, noted in the following reference, only 6 percent of the successful exsmokers felt that weight gain was a problem when they quit smoking.
ASH (Action on Smoking and Health) Women and Smoking Group. **Women and Smoking. A Handbook for Action.** Health Education Council: London, England, 1986, p.10.

12. False. The lung cancer rate is expected to surpass that of breast cancer in women in the 1980s. The sharp rise in lung

cancer rates in women is similar to, but steeper (or increasing faster) than, that seen for men 25 years earlier.

Source: United States Public Health Service. **The Health Consequences of Smoking for Women. A Report of the Surgeon General**. U.S. Department of Health and Human Services: Washington, D.C.,1980.

1981 - The Changing Cigarette

True-False Statements

__13. Reported tar and nicotine levels are measured on machines and these may not reflect the level of these substances the smoker takes into his or her body.

__14. Tobacco manufacturers do not have to report the identity of flavorings and additives used in cigarettes, and the health consequences of burning and inhaling them is unknown.

__15. Tobacco smoke is made up of gases and small particles, but the poisonous substances are only found in the gases.

__16. Nicotine is an addictive drug, but it is not connected with the heart disease or cancer associated with cigarette smoking.

__17. Smokers who use filter-tipped, lower tar and nicotine cigarettes have rates of lung and larynx cancer similar to nonsmokers.

__18. The increased use by smokers of filter-tipped, lower tar and nicotine cigarettes has clearly been shown to decrease the incidence of heart disease related to smoking.

__19. Nicotine and carbon monoxide in tobacco smoke have an effect on the body which may lead to diseases of the heart and blood vessels.

__20. If tobacco smoke is held first in the mouth before it is inhaled, it has less effect on the airways than if it is inhaled directly.

__21. A lower amount of tar and nicotine in cigarettes has not been shown to alter the effects of smoking on the unborn baby.

__22. Filter-tipped cigarettes have proven to be popular.

Answers

13. True. Over the years between 1950 and 1980, filters were added to many of the cigarettes sold in North America and tar and nicotine levels were lowered while more flavorings and chemical additives were included in cigarettes. The lowered tar concentration was brought about through altering tobacco plant genetics, cultivation and processing practices, and the paper and filtering system used in the cigarette.

Although these changes resulted in lowered tar measurements of cigarettes in laboratory tests using smoking machines, people who smoke tend to smoke more cigarettes, increase the volume of smoke inhaled and cover the holes provided for the filtering system. As a result, the lower tar cigarettes may, in reality, not result in a lower risk of disease.

14. True. Even though tar levels were lowered in cigarettes, other parts of the gas phase in the smoke may have increased. This is especially true of the additives and flavorings used to make these cigarettes more attractive to consumers. The health effects related to the burning and inhaling of these additives and flavorings is unknown, although some available for use are known or suspected cancer-producing substances.

Tobacco manufacturers are not yet required to report what additives or flavorings are used to produce cigarettes. Most major studies are of people who have smoked longer and have, therefore, smoked the older, unfiltered cigarettes with fewer additives and flavorings. The health consequences of smoking the "new" cigarettes are as yet unknown.

15. False. Tobacco and tobacco smoke are made up of at least 2000 identified substances. (This number of substances was given in the 1981 Surgeon General's Report. As noted in Chapter 2, by 1984, 3800 substances had been identified in tobacco smoke). Tobacco smoke is made up of both a mixture of gases, called the gas phase, and very small particles, called particulate matter which consists of nicotine, water and tar. Many suspected or known poisonous agents have been found

in both the gas phase and particulate matter found in ETS.

16. False. Nicotine appears to be the most important fast-acting drug in tobacco smoke. It increases blood pressure and the heart rate. Nicotine may cause the platelets in the blood to be more sticky and form clots more easily than they normally do.

Nicotine also helps the formation of tobacco-specific nitrosamines which are strong cancer-producing agents. Nitrosamines are formed while the tobacco is cured and fermented, as well as when it is burned. When used properly, filters can help to remove nitrosamines from mainstream tobacco smoke received by the smoker.

Nicotine itself may also produce cancer when working with other agents. It, therefore, may be a co-carcinogen.

It appears that the ability of tobacco to produce cancer is related to the amount of nicotine in the particulate matter. An increasing cancer-producing rate is found with an increasing concentration of nicotine.

Polycyclic aromatic hydrocarbons are another class of cancer initiators found in tobacco smoke. Of these, benzo[a]pyrene, which is formed when tobacco is burned, may be the most important. It also appears to act with nicotine to produce cancer.

17. False. Cigarettes which are filter-tipped and contain lower levels of tar and nicotine produce lower rates of cancer in the lung and larynx than do higher tar and nicotine cigarettes but they still result in a much higher rate of cancer than when cigarettes are not used at all.

It has not been shown that lower tar and nicotine content of cigarettes either increases or decreases the incidence of other types of cancer associated with smoking.

18. False. Coronary heart disease rates increase with the amount of cigarettes smoked daily and decrease when smoking ceases. The use of filters and lower levels of tar and nicotine has not had a clearly identified effect on the incidence of heart and blood vessel disease associated with smoking.

19. True. Nicotine and carbon monoxide are the constituents in tobacco smoke that have been identified as having the most

effect on cardiovascular disease. Cigarettes with low tar yields may not have lower nicotine or carbon dioxide yields. This is especially true when taking into account the way smokers may change their smoking behavior when using low yield cigarettes (for example, inhaling more deeply, using more cigarettes).

Carbon monoxide may allow lipids (fats) to go through blood vessel walls more easily, which would promote atherosclerosis (or the formation of accumulations of lipid material on the blood vessels walls). This may gradually result in a narrowing or blockage in the blood vessel where blood cannot flow through. This can cause heart attacks and other circulatory problems.

Cigarettes with unperforated filters allow lower levels of nicotine and tar to be expelled into mainstream smoke but do not decrease the level of carbon monoxide. Perforated filters do help to decrease the level of carbon monoxide, but they decrease the level of this gas much less than the proportionate decrease in the levels of the nicotine and tar.

20. True. The individual's pattern of smoking is important in determining how the smoke will affect the lungs and airways. If the smoke is first held in the mouth and then inhaled, the effect is less on the airways than when the smoke is inhaled directly.

If people who use cigarettes with lower nicotine and tar content in the smoke compensate by inhaling more deeply and/or smoke more cigarettes, they may actually increase their risk of developing obstructive airway disease.

21. True. The effects of smoking on pregnancy and the unborn baby have not been shown to either increase or decrease with the use of low-level nicotine and tar cigarettes compared to high-level ones.

22. True. The use of filter-tipped cigarettes rose from 1.4 percent in 1950 to 91.7 percent in 1979 in the United States. In the decade from 1968 to 1978 the tar content of the average cigarette decreased by 32.2 percent and the nicotine content declined by 25.6 percent (using information gathered on smoking machines).

Source: United States Public Health Service. **The Health**

Consequences of Smoking. The Changing Cigarette. A Report of the Surgeon General. U.S. Department of Health and Human Services: Washington, D.C., 1981.

1982 - Cancer and Smoking Cessation

True-False Statements

__23. A man who smokes is twice as likely to die of cancer than a man who does not smoke.

__24. Lung cancer is the only type of cancer for which cigarette smoking is the major cause.

__25. Fifteen years after a person has quit smoking, his or her risk of dying of lung cancer is still much higher than that of a nonsmoker.

__26. Cancer of the bladder, kidney and pancreas can be related to smoking behavior.

__27. Most of the millions of exsmokers have quit with the use of organized cessation programs.

__28. A new exsmoker needs to plan ahead as to how he or she will cope without cigarettes, in order to quit successfully.

__29. Cutting down gradually on the number of cigarettes smoked is the best cessation strategy.

Answers

23. True. The overall rate of cancer deaths for male smokers is about double that of nonsmokers. The rate of cancer deaths for female smokers is about 30 percent higher than that of women who do not smoke. This percentage for women smokers is rising as more women are affected by the long-term consequences of smoking.

24. False. Cigarette smoking is the major cause of lung cancer in North America but it is also the major cause of cancer of the mouth, larynx (voice box), and esophagus.

25. False. After 15 years of not smoking, an exsmoker's risk

of dying of lung cancer is only slightly more than that of a nonsmoker.

26. True. Cigarette smoking can contribute to the development of cancer of the bladder, kidney and pancreas. It appears that the nitrosamines found in tobacco smoke are important cancer-causing agents which can affect specific body organs.

27. False. Ninety-five percent of the people who have quit smoking have done so without using an organized cessation program. Most current smokers who want to quit smoking would prefer a method which they can use on their own.

28. True. The exsmoker needs to develop skill in how to deal with feelings of frustration, anxiety, anger and depression without turning to a cigarette. He or she also has to develop skill in handling social situations where there is pressure for him or her to return to smoking. People who are supportive of the person's decision not to smoke can improve the exsmoker's success rate.

29. False. Quitting "cold turkey" (or abruptly quitting smoking) appears to be more effective than gradually cutting down on the number of cigarettes smoked each day.

Source: United States Public Health Service. **The Health Consequences of Smoking. Cancer. A Report of the Surgeon General.** U.S. Department of Health and Human Services: Washington, D.C., 1982.

1983 - Diseases of the Heart and Blood Vessels

True-False Statements

__30. More people who smoke die prematurely of heart disease than cancer.

__31. A high level of cholesterol in the blood is the most commonly found risk factor associated with heart disease.

__32. People who smoke two packs of cigarettes a day have a 200 percent greater risk of dying of coronary heart disease (for example, from a heart attack) than nonsmokers.

__33. Cigarette smoking appears to be associated with athero-sclerosis which leads to narrowing and blockages in the blood vessels.

__34. Cigarette smoking increases the risk of sudden death.

__35. Unless smoking habits change, 1 percent of all persons now alive in North America may die prematurely of heart disease associated with cigarette smoking.

__36. Strokes may be associated with cigarette smoking.

__37. Blood clots in the legs and aortic aneurysms (where the wall of the major artery from the heart ruptures) are seen more frequently in people who smoke.

__38. People who have quit smoking have reduced their risk of death from heart attacks.

Answers

30. True. Approximately 30 percent of all deaths are due to coronary heart disease. It is the single most important cause of death in North America. More people die of coronary heart disease than die of all types of cancer.

It is estimated that 30 percent, or more, of the deaths from coronary heart disease can be attributed to smoking. These numbers are particularly important when it is known that the age at which people are dying of coronary heart disease is decreasing.

Other cardiovascular diseases such as strokes, peripheral vascular disease (especially in the blood vessels of the legs), aortic atheroslerosis (formation of fatty deposits on the wall of the major artery leading from the heart), and other vascular problems are more common in people who smoke.

31. False. Of the three main risk factors associated with coronary heart disease (cigarette smoking, high blood pressure and a high level of cholesterol in the blood), the one which is most prevalent in the population is cigarette smoking.

The risk of developing and dying from coronary heart disease increases with the number of cigarettes smoked per day, the number of years of smoking behavior, and the degree of inhalation. Also, the younger the person was when he or she started smoking, the higher the risk of coronary heart disease later in life.

32. True. People who smoke have a 70 percent greater chance of dying from coronary heart disease than nonsmokers and heavy smokers, who use more than two packs a day, have an almost 200 percent greater risk.

33. True. Atherosclerosis is the formation of lesions or patches of fat-containing material on or in the walls of blood vessels which can lead to blockages of the blood flow through the vessels.

Cigarette smoking appears to increase the likelihood of lesions being formed and speeds up the process on the walls of arteries, especially the aorta leading from the heart.

There is some evidence that cigarette smoking changes the levels of cholesterol in the blood in such a way that atherosclerosis will increase.

34. True. Cigarette smoking increases the risk of sudden death by two to four times. The risk is greater as the number of cigarettes smoked per day increases.

35. False. Unless smoking habits change, 10 percent of all persons now alive in North America may die prematurely of heart disease associated with cigarette smoking. After quitting smoking for 10 years, exsmokers who smoked less than a pack a day have a risk of coronary heart disease similar to that of people who have never smoked.

36. True. Cerebrovascular disease (for example, strokes) may be associated with cigarette smoking, especially when it occurs at a younger age. The risk of hemorrhage in the brain is greatly increased in women who smoke and take birth control pills. The risk is somewhat less for women who smoke but do not take birth control pills.

37. True. Cigarette smoking is the most important risk factor for peripheral vascular disease which is usually due to atherosclerosis - a narrowing or blockage of an artery in the legs. The disease may be mild (for example, pain in the leg brought

on by exercise and relieved by rest) to severe (for example, ulcers on the leg and gangrene).

People who smoke are more likely than nonsmokers to die from a rupture of the wall of their aorta, which is the major artery from the heart. The rupture occurs at an aneurysm, or weakened area of the blood vessel wall, caused by degeneration or inflammatory destruction of the wall.

38. True. Those people who have quit smoking have a substantially decreased risk of death from coronary heart disease compared to when they were smoking. Overall, they tend to live longer than if they had not quit.

Source: United States Public Health Service. **The Health Consequences of Smoking. Cardiovascular Disease. A Report of the Surgeon General**. U.S. Department of Health and Human Services: Washington, D.C., 1983.

1984 - Chronic Obstructive Lung Disease

True-False Statements

__39. Cigarette smoking is the major cause of chronic obstructive lung disease (COLD), which includes both chronic bronchitis and emphysema.

__40. Changes in the airways of the respiratory tract do not occur until many years after a person has started to smoke.

__41. The risk of death from COLD is greatly decreased soon after a person quits smoking.

__42. A person who smokes cigarettes may have more difficulty fighting off infections.

__43. Cigarette smoking affects the mechanism which cleans the airways of the respiratory tract.

Answers

39. True. Chronic obstructive lung disease (COLD) consists of three separate, but related, disease processes. They are: chronic excess secretion of mucus in the respiratory airways resulting in a chronic cough, chronic bronchitis (thickening of

the walls, and narrowing of the airways with resulting difficulty in breathing out), and emphysema (abnormal expansion of the air sacs in the lungs and destruction of their walls).

Cigarette smoking is the major cause of chronic obstructive lung disease in both men and women. Death from COLD results after many years of disability and limitation of the person's activities.

40. False. The effects on the respiratory tract begin early as shown in research experiments where, by the age of 25 years, there were measurable differences in the amount of air that smokers and nonsmokers could breath out. Only a small percentage of smokers develop severe emphysema but in older age groups, mild or moderate emphysema is present in most smokers.

Eighty to 90 percent of chronic obstructive lung disease is attributable to cigarette smoking. Abnormalities in the functioning of small airways show up a few years after the person starts to smoke. These gradually increase with age, the length of the time the person smokes, and the amount the person smokes. These abnormalities are related to inflammation in the airways caused by tobacco smoke.

41. False. Even 20 years after quitting smoking, the risk of dying of COLD for exsmokers does not decline to equal that of nonsmokers.

Pipe and cigar smokers also experience an increased risk of COLD compared to nonsmokers but not to the same extent as cigarette smokers.

42. True. Cigarette smoke may depress the body's ability to form antibodies to fight off infections.

43. True. The walls of the respiratory tract are coated with mucus and lined with cilia (or fine hairs). Small, foreign particles stick to the mucus and the cilia then move the mucus upward toward the mouth where it is either coughed up or swallowed. This is the system by which the airways are kept clean.

Both the particulate and gas phases of cigarette smoke are poisonous to the cilia. Also, cigarette smoking causes the production of an excessive amount of mucus which the cilia cannot handle. The system used to clean the airways is therefore impaired by long-term exposure to cigarette smoke.

Source: United States Public Health Service. **The Health Consequences of Smoking. Chronic Obstructive Lung Disease. A Report of the Surgeon General.** U.S. Department of Health and Human Services: Washington, D.C., 1984.

1985 - Cancer and Chronic Lung Disease in the Work-place

True-False Statements

__44. The work-place environment can affect the rate of nonsmoking and smoking for employees.

__45. Lung cancer is associated with exposure to asbestos and with cigarette smoking. Where these factors exist together, the risk of lung cancer is additive; that is, the total risk is now the level of risk of lung cancer associated with asbestos exposure, added to the level of risk associated with cigarette smoking.

__46. For the majority of workers who smoke, other hazards in the work-place are more likely to cause death and disability than will their smoking.

__47. A greater percentage of blue-collar workers than white-collar workers are exsmokers.

__48. Cigarette smoking is a more important factor in producing chronic bronchitis than is exposure to coal dust, grain, or silica dust.

Answers

44. True. Although most people begin to smoke during their school years, some start when they enter the work-force. The work-place environment can either discourage or support and encourage smoking. An atmosphere where cessation and nonsmoking are encouraged should be considered as part of a work-place safety program.

45. False. Exposure to certain occupational hazards (for example, asbestos) is known to cause lung cancer and chronic

lung disease. If workers exposed to these substances are also smokers, their risk of these diseases is **multiplied.** A nonsmoker exposed to asbestos has a risk of lung cancer five times that of a nonsmoker not exposed. A smoker has 10 times the risk of lung cancer. However, a smoker who is also exposed to asbestos has a risk of lung cancer 50 times that of a nonsmoker who is not exposed to asbestos. The danger increases dramatically when more than one hazard is present.

46. False. For the majority of workers who smoke cigarettes, their smoking behavior is more likely to cause death and disability than any other hazards in their work-place environment.

47. False. More white-collar workers are exsmokers. Blue-collar workers are more likely to be current smokers than white-collar workers. Blue-collar workers are also more likely to have started smoking at an earlier age.

48. True. Chronic bronchitis is associated with exposure to coal, grain, silica, the welding environment and, to a lesser degree, sulphur dioxide and cement. Cigarette smoking is a more important factor in producing chronic bronchitis, but when smokers are also exposed to these work-place hazards their risk is multiplied.

Source: United States Public Health Service. **The Health Consequences of Smoking. Cancer and Chronic Lung Disease in the Work-place. A Report of the Surgeon General.** U.S. Department of Health and Human Services: Washington, D.C., 1985.

1986 - The Health Consequences of Using Smokeless Tobacco

True-False Statements

__49. The use of smokeless tobacco has increased recently, especially by young people in the United States.

__50. Smokeless tobacco (for example, snuff, chewing tobacco) is a healthy alternative to cigarette smoking.

Answers

49. True. In 1986, an additional report on the health consequences of the use of smokeless tobacco was written, because this substance was being widely promoted in the United States and its use was increasing, especially among young people.

50. False. The committee which studied the problem determined that smokeless tobacco was not a safe alternative to cigarette smoking and, in fact, was associated with cancer of the mouth and addiction to nicotine.

As the exposure to nicotine is similar with the use of both smokeless tobacco and cigarettes, its effect with each type of use may also be the same. Although the effects of smokeless tobacco have not been as well studied, it may also contribute to the incidence of coronary heart disease, peripheral vascular disease, high blood pressure, and stomach ulcers. If used by pregnant women, it may also increase the risk of illness and death in unborn babies.

Studies indicate that risk of cancer is increased at the site of exposure to snuff. Frequently used sites include the mouth and nose. The risk of cancer of the cheek and gum can increase as much as fifty times in long-term snuff users compared to those who do not use snuff.

Some potent cancer-causing agents are found in smokeless tobacco. These include nitrosamines, polycyclic aromatic hydrocarbons, and radiation-emitting polonium. Nitrosamines in some smokeless tobacco have been found to be at levels 100 times that allowed in food.

Source: United States Public Health Service. **The Health Consequences of Using Smokeless Tobacco. A Report of the Advisory Committee to the Surgeon General.** U.S. Department of Health and Human Services: Washington, D.C., 1986.

Appendix B : ICBC Staff Memo on Their Work-place Policy

The following information was contained in the memo sent out to all employees of the Insurance Corporation of British Columbia on July 5, 1985 under the signature of the president and chief executive officer of the company.

Subject: CORPORATE SMOKING POLICY

The staff committee established to recommend a corporate policy on smoking in corporation premises has now submitted its final report.

The policy adopted as a result of the committee's recommendation is attached, along with supportive information presented in a question-and-answer format. This will clarify the rationale for the policy.

Please note that the policy will come into effect on October 1, 1985.

The principal factors influencing the setting of this policy were:
- corporate concern for the health of our employees – both smokers and nonsmokers;
- medical and other scientific evidence of the effects of smoke in the work-place; and
- the staff survey which overwhelmingly endorsed the need for this policy.

The staff committee did an excellent job and I commend them for their efforts.

Written comments on the policy are welcome. Please send them to: Smoking Policy Committee, Head Office

Insurance Corporation of British Columbia
Corporate Smoking Policy

SUBJECT: Smoking in ICBC premises.

GOAL: To provide employees with a smoke-free work environment.

TIMING: The date upon which the stated goal is achieved is as yet undetermined, and subject to further review by the general staff population. The effective date of the policy which follows is October 1, 1985.

POLICY:
LOCATIONS OTHER THAN HEAD OFFICE
Smoking will be permitted in the lunchroom. No smoking in all other inside facilities of ICBC buildings or premises.
HEAD OFFICE
Smoking will be permitted in a designated area of the cafeteria and in designated employee pause areas (lounges and coffee/lunch rooms). No smoking in all other inside facilities of the building.

APPLICABILITY: All occupants of ICBC premises.

IMPLEMENTATION: ICBC's policy on smoking will be made clear by the following:
A. "No Smoking" signs shall be prominently posted on all entrances to ICBC facilities and in every "public" area. While it is intended that all occupants of ICBC premises will respect our policy, the individual preferences of visiting members of the public will prevail.
B. Head Office pause areas in which smoking is permitted shall be designated by appropriate signage.
C. Upon request, managers of locations other than Head Office will provide, if possible, an alternative lunch facility for non-smokers. Should no such alternative exist, the employee's own work station may be appropriate.

RESPONSIBILITIES: The manager of each Head Office department or ICBC premise is responsible for implementing this policy and, together with supervisory personnel, for orienting employees to the importance of complying with the policy.

ICBC SMOKING POLICY QUESTIONS AND ANSWERS

Your Smoking Policy Committee read all written comments received in the recent employee survey on smoking in the work-place. Following are a number of the issues raised by staff, as well as supportive information to the corporate policy. While the answers are specific with respect to ICBC's policy, in a general sense they represent the consolidated experience and conclusions of medical experts and progressive organizations throughout North America.

1. Q: Why is the long-term goal a "smoke-free" environment?
A: As long as some smoking continues, the health hazards still exist on an involuntary basis.

2. Q: When will the corporation go "smoke-free"?
A: This goal has no date attached to it, and would be reviewed again prior to implementation.

3. Q: Why didn't the policy ban smoking entirely in ICBC facilities?
A: A significant number of employees saw this as a viable position. However, it is recognized the new policy will present a hardship for some smokers, and designated areas afford assistance to help with the adjustment.

4. Q: Why not designate areas for work stations?
A: Work stations represent the critical element of a meaningful policy. Because virtually all our premises function on recycled air, the segregation of smokers and nonsmokers in an open area will provide some direct-irritant relief only. We all still breathe the same air. In view of this being the place where we must spend most of the work day, the position taken was considered one that could not be compromised.

5. Q: How did you determine in which areas smoking would be permitted?
A: A review of corporate facilities confirmed that virtually all

ICBC premises have a room separated from the general work area for coffee and lunch breaks. Many of these are on outside walls, offering the potential for externally-ventilating exhaust systems. In an endeavour to eliminate smoking at the work stations and all other common-use areas in which employees have no choice but to attend, this seemed a reasonable compromise.

6. Q: Won't the lunchrooms become "blue" with smoke?
A: The incidence of smoking in lunchrooms beyond normal break periods should be no greater than prior to the policy. Nonsmokers outside Head Office desiring an alternative should pursue the matter with their manager.

7. Q: How do we handle visitors that smoke in our facilities?
A: With tact and diplomacy. You should courteously advise visitors of our policy, but by no means engage in a confrontation or make them feel uncomfortable should they choose to smoke. The vast majority of smokers will respect the policy if presented effectively.

8. Q: Does the corporation have the legal right to interfere with my freedom to smoke?
A: The corporation is not asking smokers to quit. However, the right to clean air must take precedence over the right to smoke at the work-place. Although it is a relatively new legal issue, a clear trend is developing which upholds the right to a safe, healthful, smoke-free work environment, and underscores the duty of an employer to ensure this right.

9.Q: What about violation of the policy?
A: There have been areas provided in which smoking is permitted. However, should the occasion arise, standard progressive discipline procedures would apply.

10. Q: What can I do if a fellow employee ignores the policy?
A: Politely ask the employee to respect corporate policy by limiting his or her smoking to designated areas. Should the employee fail to respond, speak to your supervisor or manager, or someone from Health Services or Employee Relations.

11.Q: Does the policy extend to corporate vehicles?

A: As a formal inclusion to the policy this is not practical or seen to be necessary. Wherever possible those responsible for corporate vehicles will try to designate a number of vehicles for use by smokers. Leaving vehicles in a general state of cleanliness and readiness for the next user is only common courtesy.

12. Q: Why can't the problem of second-hand smoke be addressed through improved building ventilation?
A: Second-hand smoke contains both a particulate and gaseous component. There has not yet been a filtration and recycling system developed that effectively addresses the gaseous component. Apart from the equipment costs necessary to facilitate sufficient air exchange, it has been estimated that the 100 to 200 exchanges per hour required to remove those gases would cause gale-force winds in the work-place.

13. Q: Are other B.C. companies taking similar steps on smoking in the work-place?
A: Yes. Established policies already exist at B.C. Telephone, Vancouver General Hospital, B.C. Rail, and VanCity Savings Credit Union. The corporation has received numerous enquiries from public and private organizations on the development of our policy.

14. Q: Didn't recent air quality tests at Head Office rate us as "excellent"?
A: Yes. However, these tests measured only a few selected gases – carbon monoxide, carbon dioxide, formaldehyde, nitrogen oxides, and oxygen – and ignore some of the most toxic gases found in tobacco smoke. In any event there is a strong position to be made that the only acceptable level of exposure to tobacco smoke is zero.

15. Q: Why should the corporation support the costs of cessation programs?
A: The corporation recognizes the difficulty of adjustment some smokers may face with this new policy. In an effort to assist those who invest personal time into a cessation program, the corporation is willing to provide financial support as a sound investment in our employees' health.

16. Q: This is a change in policy from when I was first hired – is this fair?
A: Yes, things do change. For example, hours of work have been modified to reflect changed service levels to the public and agents which has affected many employees. There very likely will always be changes to one degree or another in corporate policy.

17. Q: Why not let each individual department or work facility determine their own policy?
A: Any corporate policy, to be effective, must be equitable and consistent across the corporation. B.C. Telephone tried an approach of individual department preference and found it to be very unsatisfactory. They are currently reviewing their policy with an eye to uniform consistency. This is not an issue in which the majority preference of a particular department or location should prevail over clean air. The balance of such preference could shift every time an employee transfers in or out of the work unit. What we are trying to achieve is an improved standard of work environment for all employees of the corporation.

18. Q: With so many unhealthy lifestyles, why pick out cigarette smoking as deserving of a corporate policy?
A: Cigarette smoking differs from other habits because it affects the health of others. Cigarette smoke is one of the major health and safety issues in the work-place today.

19. Q: Will ICBC have a discriminatory hiring policy as a result of this smoking policy?
A: No. We are not asking employees to quit smoking. We are restricting their opportunities to do so at work. Prospective new employees would be advised of our policy as part of the selection process.

20.Q: Under the new policy will smokers be allowed to take as many breaks as they wish?
A: No. The existing policy on breaks is still in effect.

21. Q: Does the policy include private offices?
A: Yes, for two reasons:
•Air quality – because we all wind up breathing the same

recycled air, the filtration of which does not eliminate the hazard.

•Equity – because it is not fair to allow a manager to smoke in a private office while those who work in a more open environment are prohibited from smoking at their work station. Office smoking also presents a health hazard to co-workers who must come into the office to conduct business.

22. Q: How does this help productivity, operating costs, or the settlement of claims?

A: This was never the intent or anticipated result of the new policy. It is not expected to harm these areas either, but the policy is in response to problems, concerns, and possible health impact on passive as well as active smokers.

23. Q: Will we hear more on this subject?

A: Yes. The corporation intends to monitor not only our own work-place, but the activity of other employers. We will continue to communicate with you on the topic and intend to take another survey in the future.

Appendix C : Sources of Information and Referral

The following are sources which, along with state, provincial, or territorial health departments may be useful to you in obtaining further information on protection from environmental tobacco smoke, prevention of smoking and smoking cessation. Many of the national health organizations also have local and regional offices.

CANADA

Canadian Cancer Society
77 Bloor Street West, Suite 1702,
Toronto, Ontario M5S 3A1
Phone: Contact local unit

Canadian Council on Smoking and Health
1565 Carling Avenue, Suite 400,
Ottawa, Ontario K1Z 8R1
Phone: (613) 722-3419

Canadian Headquarters, Seventh Day Adventists
Health and Temperance Department,
1148 Kings Street East,
Oshawa, Ontario L1H 1H8
Phone: (416)433-0011 or local church

Canadian Heart Foundation
1 Nicholas Street, Suite 1200,
Ottawa, Ontario K1N 7B7
Phone: (613) 237-4361 or provincial office

Canadian Lung Association
75 Albert Street, Suite 908,
Ottawa, Ontario K1P 5E7
Phone: (613) 237-1208 or provincial/territorial office

Health and Welfare Canada
4th Floor, Jeanne Mance Building, Tunney's Pasture,
Ottawa, Ontario K1A 1B4
Phone: Tobacco Programs Unit, Health Promotion
(613)957-8332
Tobacco Products Unit, Environmental Health
(613)954-0151

Members of Legislative Assembly
Parliament Buildings, capital city of your province
Phone: local constituency office number in telephone directory

Members of Parliament
Parliament Buildings, Ottawa, Ontario (no postage required)
Phone: Local constituency office number in telephone directory
For name of local MP, phone toll-free 1-800-267-2380

Nonsmokers' Rights Association
344 Bloor Street West, Suite 308,
Toronto, Ontario M5S 1W9
Phone: (416)928-2900

Physicians for a Smoke-Free Canada
Box 4849, Station E,
Ottawa, Ontario K1S 5J1

UNITED STATES

Action on Smoking and Health (ASH),
2013 H Street, N.W.,
Washington, D.C. 20006

American Cancer Society
90 Park Avenue,
New York, New York 10016
Phone:(212)599-8200 or toll-free 1-800-4-CANCER

American Heart Association
National Center, 7320 Greenville Avenue,
Dallas, Texas 75231
Phone:(214)750-5300

American Lung Association
1740 Broadway,
New York, New York 10019
Phone:(212)315-8700

Americans for Nonsmokers Rights
2054 University Avenue, Suite 500,
Berkeley, California 94704
Phone:(415)841-3032
(legislation, especially at state level, and prevention)

Center for Health Promotion and Education
Centers for Disease Control,
Building 3, 1600 Clifton Road NE,
Atlanta, Georgia 30333

Clean Air Associates
25 Deaconess Road,
Boston, Massachusetts 02215
Phone: (617) 566-7758
(workplace policies)

Coalition on Smoking or Health
1607 New Hampshire Ave., 4th Floor,
Washington D.C. 20009
Phone: (202)234-9375
(group which lobbies at the national level)

Congresspersons
U.S. House of Representatives,
Washington, B.C. 20515
Phone: (202)224-3121

Doctors Ought to Care (DOC)
HH-101, Medical College of Georgia,
Augusta, Georgia 30912
Phone:(404)721-2269

Environmental Improvement Association
109 Chestnut Street,
Salem, New Jersey 08079
(workplace policies)

General Conference of Seventh-Day Adventists
Health and Temperance Department,
6840 Eastern Avenue NW,
Washington, D.C. 20012
Phone:(202)722-6700

National Heart, Lung and Blood Institute
Smoking Education Program,
Building 31, Room 4A-21, 9000 Rockville Pike,
Bethesda, Maryland 20892

National Institute of Child Health and Human Development
Department of Health and Human Services,
Building 31, Room 2A-32, 9000 Rockville Pike,
Bethesda, Maryland 20892

Public Inquiries, Office on Smoking and Health
Park Building, Room 1-10, 5600 Fishers Lane,
Rockville, Maryland 20857
Phone:(301)443-1575 or (301)443-1690

Senators
United States Senate,
Washington, D.C. 20510
Phone:(202)224-3121

INTERNATIONAL

Seventh World Conference on Tobacco and Health,
Perth, Western Australia, Spring 1990.
For information contact:
Michael Daube, Health Promotion and Education Services,
Health Department of Western Australia,
60 Beaufort St., Perth, W.A. 6000
Australia.

Index

Comments

We are interested in learning about your experiences in working toward a smoke-free goal. Please return your comments to the address below.

What was your initial goal?

____

____

Did you use some of the ideas in this book? What worked for you and what did not?

____

____

____

What sources of information and resources did you find useful?

____

____

Did you try out some new ideas that worked? If so, please share them.

____

____

How could this book have been more helpful to you?

____

____

Return to: Qualy Publishing, P.O. Box 6399, Victoria, B.C. CANADA V8N 2A2

Order Form

This book is available from leading bookstores, or directly from the publisher by using this order form.

Please send _____copies of **The Smoke-Free Guide** at $14.95 per copy for a cost of: ________
(Cost is $11 per copy for 10 or more copies)

Add 10% for shipping costs: + ________
(For orders of over $150, add 7% for shipping)

Total Due: = ________

____Payment enclosed. Note: Orders from individuals and all orders under $40 must be prepaid.

____Please bill us. Purchase Order #___________

Orders from the United States: Please pay in U.S. funds.
Overseas orders: Please add 10 percent to the Total Due and prepay in Canadian funds.

I understand that I may return any book for a refund if not satisfied.

Ship to:
Name:____

Address:____

______________________________Zip/Postal Code__________

Date:___________

Return to:

Qualy Publishing
P.O. Box 6399,Victoria, B.C. CANADA V8P 5M3